I Have A Purpose

Melissa Ford

Print ISBN: 978-1-09832-882-5

eBook ISBN: 978-1-09832-883-2

Table of Contents

Introduction

I have never had the desire to write a book. If the thought ever crossed my mind, I would never have imagined writing one about myself. I absolutely love to read and, when time allows, I can read for hours. My idea of a perfect day is relaxing on the beach or curled up on the couch with a good book to read.

My friends and family know that I don't like to talk about myself or be the center of attention. I would rather be just another face in the crowd than to be noticed. When God began stirring in my heart to write a book about myself and some of my life experiences, I thought, "That can't be God! Why would He want me to talk about myself?" Negative thoughts began to creep into my mind and I told myself, "I'm not interesting enough. I haven't lived enough to write about anything important. Who would want to pick up my book and read it?" But those fears were not coming from God. God had a different plan and a calling on my life to bless others. Sometimes our human minds cannot see the greater plans God has for us. I have learned over the course of my life, especially during my journey of writing this book, that I am only wasting my time trying to figure things out myself. I need to leave all of my worries and fears in God's hands.

Something happened one particular Saturday when my husband and I were driving to Dallas to visit our kids and grandbaby. On this day, God began giving me a vision about this book. He gave me the scriptures, the title, and most of what is included in this book. I became so overwhelmed with emotion that I started crying in the passenger seat. After hearing me sniffle a few times, my husband looked over and asked me what was wrong. I couldn't talk from the weepy tears and the biggest lump I have ever had in my throat. He asked me if I was okay, to which I nodded, "Yes." He asked if I was feeling bad, but all I could do was shake my head, "No." He was puzzled and couldn't figure out why I was crying and why I couldn't talk. Eventually, I was able to recover enough to gather a few words and I told him that I would explain more later. I turned back towards the passenger side window and continued to look outside. God continued to give me more material and kept reminding me of things in my life that I had forgotten about or hidden in the deepest part of my mind. There were things He wanted me to include that I had not thought about in several years.

In *I Have a Purpose*, the stories I share are only a few events from my life. These are things that have happened to me and things from which God has delivered me. While I have changed the names of some of the characters in this book to protect the identity of some people who may not wish to have their past written about, I want my readers to understand one immutable fact: **It doesn't matter what you've done or are doing. It doesn't matter where you are or have been in life - past, present or future. God can and will turn things around for you.**

This book was written with the singular purpose of showing how powerful God is, how He pulled me out of some circumstances, and how He rescued and healed me from so many things.

He literally turned my life around and blessed me more than I could have ever imagined. My story tells how, through all the circumstances of my life, I found MY purpose - and He can do the same for you. I hope you enjoy reading, *I Have a Purpose.*

Acknowledgements

This book would not have been possible without some of my closest loved ones.

A big thank you to my best friend and wonderful husband, Robert. You are my better half! Your support and encouragement mean the world to me. Your patience and willingness to put up with me and all my craziness while trying to put this book together has not gone unnoticed. You have been by my side for 28 years and you have been there to witness some of these occurrences in my life. I don't know how I would have made it this far without you by my side. I love doing life and growing old with you. I love you so much!

A much deserved thank you also goes to my children! You were both my motivation in completing this book.

Kris, you have been one of my biggest encouragers during this time. Every time we discussed the book, you made me more enthusiastic and excited to complete the book. Your words of wisdom and love made me feel like I could conquer the world. Thank you for giving me pep talks when I was having doubts about myself and my writing abilities. Your advice on the book, and the help with editing and proofreading have been enormous. Hearing the words, "I'm proud of you, Mom!" really turned my heart to mush. I love you, son.

Melanie, you have also been one of my biggest cheerleaders and encouragers during this time. I couldn't have done this without you! The look of excitement when I read the first page to you really got me excited to get the book written. Every time we talked about it and you asked me if it was finished, and every time you told me that you couldn't wait to read it was a big push for me to keep going! You don't know how many times I wanted to quit, but I didn't, because of you. Thank you for the proofreading, suggestions, and editing. There is no way for you to know how much your opinions and suggestions helped me. Thank you for always knowing what to say when I needed to hear it most. I love you, baby girl.

I would also like to thank my mom and dad and my brothers in helping me remember facts and details for this book, especially of events when I was younger. My family is the best.

I love you all!

I would like to thank Lynette King for all the hours spent editing, your suggestions and encouragement. I appreciate your help so much.

I would like to thank Isaiah Shook for taking the time to read my story, editing, making suggestions, and for your help and encouragement.

I would like to thank Sarah Scott for your talent and suggestions with the book cover, you did an amazing job.

I would like to thank my friend and coworker Casey Stone for your honest feedback, and encouragement about the book and all the extra advice about following God's plans for me as an author.

I would like to thank my friend and coworker Morgan Whitehead for reading my story, and for your encouragement every time I tried to talk myself out of this book.

Chapter 1
Purpose

What is Purpose?

Purpose – (noun) the reason for which something is done or created or for which something exists; (verb) to have as one's intention or objective.

Have you ever wondered:

> Why you were created?
>
> Why do I exist?
>
> What is God's purpose for me?
>
> What if I missed my purpose?

You are not alone, my friend.

Unfortunately, so many people think that they do not have a purpose, or they fear they will never find the reason they are here. Some people might think that the life they are living *is* their purpose, but the truth is, most haven't even begun to reach their full potential.

We tend to get caught up doing the same thing every morning: going to a job that we may not like, but we stay because (we say) that's the only thing we know how to do. Sometimes, we do it because it is our comfort zone. It is so mundane, perhaps even monotonous, that we could get to work and complete our routines with our eyes closed. Before we know it, 10 or 20 years are behind us, time has flown by and we are experiencing burn out in our jobs and careers only to wonder why we aren't satisfied.

I believe the reason for this feeling is because we are not living out our purpose and, until we reach it, we will not be satisfied. I don't have all the answers or some creative way to tell you how to find your purpose. Some people search all their lives for purpose. Every year, millions of dollars are spent by people in search of purpose and meaning in their lives. They seek help from counselors, psychologists, life coaches, and preachers. However, I'm not sure they will ever find what they are truly looking for without help from the One who created them.

I can tell you from my personal experience where I have found answers. I personally believe that to find what you are looking for, you should seek God. Pray and ask God to show you what your purpose is and to prepare you to fulfill that which He has called you to do. Read the Bible for confirmation of what you think you're hearing, God will never tell you to do something that is against or contrary to His character.

God's Word talks about purpose in several scriptures. Look them up and study them. One of my favorite scriptures about purpose is in Ephesians 2:10 where it says:

We have become His poetry, a re-created people that will fulfill the destiny He has given each of us, for we are joined to Jesus, the Anointed one. Even before we were born, God planned in advance our destiny and the good works we would do to fulfill it! (The Passion Translation)

My opinion of what this scripture says is that we were all created with a purpose. When God calls us to purpose, He has already given us everything we need to accomplish that purpose. Most people will say the hardest part is trying to figure out what our gifts are, what our purpose is, and (perhaps the biggest question), how to use those gifts to fulfill our purpose and destiny.

Psalm 139:16, the scripture says,

*Before we were even born, God had planned our
days. (The Passion Translation)*

Isn't it amazing that we were thought of by God *before* we were even born?

It blows my mind to think He knew what He had planned for each and every one of us before we ever even came into this world. Take a minute and think about how many billions of people there are in this world. Now think about what that scripture says: He has a plan and purpose for every single one of us – and it was planned before we were born. WOW! God is Awesome!

There is not one of us who is more important than another. In God's eyes, we are all the same. It doesn't matter what color we are, where we came from, what our political stance is, if we are rich or poor, or even if we are Christian or not. God loves us all the same and our purpose has already been chosen by Him, specifically for us! No one else in the world can do what He has planned for US to do. It is up to us to seek God and step into our purpose.

I feel that the reason God wanted me to write this book was to use life experiences, failures, wins, and testimonies to reach people who are emotionally injured or going through situations similar to mine. God wants to use each of us to touch the lost, the broken and the lonely. There are so many people in the world who are hurting, alone, or feel like no one can relate to their pain. We must each be in prayer to recognize the lost, because THEY are our purpose.

We all have a story. You never know how your story can change another person's life, perspective, or maybe even save a life. You never know who is watching you. Some people may think you "have it all together." They may even wish they had it as good as you. But they don't know the hell you have gone through to get where you are today. If they knew your story, they might find hope for themselves and they might even think. "If it can happen for them, it can happen for me!" **Let's find our purpose!**

Chapter 2

In My Beginning

In 1967, my mom got married at the young age of 14 to her first husband with whom she had my two older brothers Lee & Ruben. They divorced and a few years later she met and fell in love with my dad in 1972. They dated for a little while and finally married in January of 1973.

My story starts in February of 1976 in Wichita Falls, Texas. My mom woke up not feeling well one morning. She was cramping, had sharp pains in her stomach, and felt sick enough to call her sister to take her to the doctor.

Several tests were run and after anxiously awaiting the results, my mom found out she was four months pregnant with me. She was shocked because she hadn't had any of the signs or symptoms of being pregnant, even though she and my dad had been trying to get pregnant for a few years. However, she was suddenly thrown into total disbelief when the doctor advised her to terminate the pregnancy because, based on his medical opinion, the cramping and pains she was feeling was because she was having a miscarriage. To be told that she was finally pregnant, but then informed she was miscarrying the child she so desired was the ultimate in emotional upheaval. My mom was a preacher's daughter and she believed in miracles. She knew that God could heal, and she knew that God could turn any negative circumstance into a blessing. Without hesitation or doubt in her mind, she told the doctor she would not end her pregnancy. She asked him what she could do to save her baby. He advised her to go home and stay on bed rest for two weeks, but if her symptoms were to get any worse, she would have no choice but to terminate.

My mom didn't have the chance to call her parents, but shortly after she arrived back home from the hospital, my grandparents showed up at her doorstep. My grandpa told her the reason they showed up without calling was because he had a feeling something was wrong. Grandpa felt like God wanted him to drop by and pray with her.

My grandpa always said God would usually reveal to him when his kids were going through tough times. My mom told him exactly what the doctor had told her. He listened as she explained, but then told he her not to accept the negative diagnosis given to her by the doctor. It wasn't that he didn't believe the doctor could be right. He just knew that God was bigger than the problem. Grandpa assured my mom that she was not going to lose her child. He knew she and my dad had been trying to get pregnant for a few years, so he told her that instead of letting fear creep in, she needed to pray about it. She needed to put the whole situation in God's hands. He told her she just had to give that child to God and let Him take care of it. As they prayed together, they claimed life for her child, that she would go full term with the pregnancy, and that her baby would be healthy. Right there in our living room, they prayed, declared, and believed in agreement that I would have life and that, from that day forward, there wouldn't be any more complications.

My mom went full term and gained more weight than in any of her other pregnancies. She gave birth to a very healthy baby girl who weighed 8 pounds and 11 ½ ounces. Of the four children she had, I was the largest at birth.

I was born and I have a purpose.

Even before I entered this world, the enemy was already trying to attack me. He knew that I would have a God-given purpose and that one day I would find it and use it to spread the Word of God. I'm grateful that my mom had faith and that God answered their prayers. Otherwise, that doctor could have talked my mom into ending my life before I even had a chance to live.

"Before I formed you in the womb I knew you [and approved of you as My chosen instrument], and before you were born I consecrated you [to Myself as My own]; I have appointed you as a prophet to the nations" Jeremiah 1:5 AMP

My mom tells me that I was a smart baby: I started walking at eight months old, was potty-trained at 11 months, by the time I was two, I knew the alphabet and was trying to sound out letters on signs and in books to make words. My mom always bragged about how sharp I was and how quickly I caught on.

However, I have to give credit where it is due. Since I was my dad's only child and my mom's only girl, there was no lack of attention from my parents or siblings during those first few years. My two older brothers who are seven and eight years older than me, respectively. I remember them reading to me, playing games with me, and talking to me like I was as old as they were, which probably helped me catch on to ideas and concepts more quickly. I tried to do and say everything they did. In fact, I was probably the "oldest" three-year-old around. I have to admit, I was pretty spoiled too! They thought I was the "greatest thing since sliced bread," that is, until they started getting in trouble when I got hurt, cried, or didn't get my way. My mom said that my brother, Ruben, even asked my grandma if there was any way to send me back where I came from since he always got in trouble because of me.

I was a typical, healthy kid until I was about four years old and I got pretty sick. Out of concern they took me to the emergency room for what my mom describes as "foaming at the mouth." It turned out to be asthma. I had so much drainage to cough out that it looked foamy. I found out just a few years ago that my brother, Lee, was extremely worried about me at the time. He thought it wasn't like me to be sick and he had never seen me in that "foaming" condition. He did the only thing he knew how to do. He prayed to God. As I laid there looking lifeless and lethargic, he prayed to God for his baby sister to live. He said he told God that if He must take someone, to take him instead. Looking back on this situation now, I realize this was just another example of our enemy, the devil, trying to steal, kill, and destroy in order to keep me from my purpose. (John 10:10)

My oldest brother, Lee, was only 12 when he asked God to spare my life. That is a big prayer for a kid that age! After a few days of medications, and most importantly my brother's prayers, I was better and back to my old self.

I have a purpose!

Chapter 3
Change is Coming

Even as a child, one can sense when the atmosphere around them starts to feel different. Things at home started to feel cold and bitter. My parents were arguing a lot, the sound of doors slamming, and yelling adults were becoming a regular occurrence in our home. Sometimes, things were being thrown at each other and hateful words were spoken toward each other. Eventually, my dad moved out.

What my parents (and most adults) don't think about is that even after an argument is over and they have forgiven each other, those words still ring loudly in their children's ears. The cussing, yelling, and hand gestures never quite leave a child's memory.

With my parent's separation, my brothers and I spent a lot of time with my grandparents, which meant a lot of time in church. They took us along for hospital visits when grandpa had to pray for the sick. We ate with them at their church member's houses, and we attended a lot of church rallies, revivals and conferences.

I was five when I asked Jesus into my heart. I remember my Sunday school teacher at my grandpa's church asking if anyone wanted to ask Jesus to be their Lord and Savior. I raised my hand

and she asked me to repeat a prayer with her and that was the beginning of my relationship with Jesus.

Back in those days, churches used to have a time during the service when people from the congregation could share a testimony or sing a song (called a "special"). I used to sing at my grandpa's church sometimes and, as I got older, I sang at other churches too. I would walk up to the front of the church with so much courage, grab the microphone, and sing with all my heart. I lost that courage and confidence as I grew older. If I were asked to do it now, I would quickly decline. Just the thought of singing in front of a crowd today makes me want to throw up. Where does our childhood courage go? Despite all the problems we had going on at home, singing about Jesus at church always brought me peace.

During that period of my life, the only time I felt happy was when we were with our grandparents – either in their home or at the many church functions. My home life was crumbling. I still got to see my dad, and even though he tried to make the best of the time we spent together, I could sense his unhappiness. I could tell he was hurting but he was trying to be tough about it. He began dealing with it the only way he knew how, but that wasn't in a good way. He was already an alcoholic, but the amount of drinking greatly increased.

For my mother, the stress of being a single parent started showing at home. She always seemed frazzled and distant, and she wasn't a happy person anymore. She and my grandparents argued a lot, too. My grandparents loved that we "had" to spend a lot of time with them. They loved being able to spoil us, but I think they were unhappy about some of the choices my mom was making. Perhaps more importantly, they knew she had gotten away from church and God.

One spring Saturday in May of 1982, my Uncle Roy, his brother-in-law, my mom, my brother Ruben, and I left Seymour, Texas, headed to Wichita Falls, Texas, which was about a 50-mile drive. At the time, I didn't know where we were going or why. I just remember my mom and grandma arguing in Spanish before we left. My mom seemed upset. I remember a comment my grandma had made about my mom being rebellious and "not living right," but at the time, I didn't understand what that meant.

Once in the car, I learned we were going out of town for my mom and uncle to sing at clubs and bars. I understand now why my grandma was so upset. She didn't want her kids out partying and singing in clubs. They were preacher's kids and she didn't want them living the party lifestyle she knew was contrary to her own beliefs and the way they were raised. However, while they were old enough to choose for themselves, she didn't want her grandkids exposed to that kind of influence.

After we left my grandparent's house, my mom began telling my uncle about the argument with my grandma. She told my uncle that the reason we kids had to come with them was because my grandma had refused to watch us. Mom said she just didn't want her to go out and have a good time.

My uncle was driving my mom's new sports car, his brother-in-law was in the passenger seat, and my mom was sitting in the back with my brother and me. I started getting sleepy in the car, as any little kid of five years old would on a road trip. Sitting in the middle of the back seat, I tried to partially lie down, but because it was a small car, this caused my brother and I to start arguing. Ruben said I was trying to hog the back seat so my mom, trying to keep the peace, had me switch places with her. I was barely getting comfortable in my new spot next to the back window, when the man in front of me began to yell at my uncle. "Watch out!" He was waving his hands in the air yelling, "He's going to hit us!"

I was sitting directly behind him wondering what in the world he was yelling about. My uncle had slowed down and stopped for a little family of badgers to cross the road, but the 18-wheeler behind us was not slowing down. Uncle Roy seemed to be deaf at the time because he wasn't moving the car. We just sat there in the middle of the road and, before he could react, the 18-wheeler slammed into our car from behind.

It is now 36 years later and still to this day, I can hear the loud crash in my head like it happened just yesterday. I can smell the rubber from the tires and see the black stripes on the highway as vivid as they were that day. I can see the face of the man who was driving the 18-wheeler. He was horrified and very apologetic. He kept shaking his head and kept saying he was sorry. The image of the bright red blood in the car and on us is still very much alive in my memory.

People from both sides of the highway started pulling over to help. They helped my brother and I get out of the back seat, but my mom just lay there – apparently lifeless. My uncle was in shock and in freak-out mode trying to figure out what to do as we all watched my mom.

My brother and I found each other in all of the chaos and hugged in relief. We both had glass in our skin and scalps from the hatchback window shattering all over us. While we had some minor cuts and bruises as well, my mom still laid inside the car as people were trying to figure out how to get her out. She honestly looked dead. She started yelling out my uncle's name and kept asking him, "Are Melissa and Ruben okay? Where are my kids?" She was laying there in a semi-conscious state but, as any mother would be, she was worried about her kids.

People were trying to distract us and talk to us to keep us from watching, but my brother and I stood there, still looking at her and watching everything. We didn't know whether she was going to live or not. It's such a weird feeling – watching someone lay there yet not knowing if this is the end for them. Everyone was saying not to move her until the ambulance got there.

After the ambulance and other emergency services arrived, they were finally able to remove her from the car. I don't remember if it was the emergency services or someone else, but we could hear people talking and whispering that she had a broken back and neck. We were all taken to the hospital in Seymour, but they decided to transfer my mom to the hospital in Wichita Falls since it was better equipped to treat the seriousness of her condition.

While my mom was in the hospital and since my parents were still separated and living in different towns, we stayed with our grandparents. After a few days, they took us to visit our mom. I remember looking carefully at her. I was curious as to why she wouldn't move her head or neck to talk to us when we walked in the door. I finally got close enough to see that, because her neck was broken, they had strapped her head to the hospital bed so she could not move it. I remember the nursing staff could turn the bed face down and I would get under the bed and look up at her and talk to her.

As I sat and listened to my grandparents and mom talk, I was lost in thought and could not figure out why this had all happened. I even felt a sense of guilt as I watched how badly she was suffering. I thought that if I had not laid down, my brother and I would not have fought and mom would not be in this condition. It never once crossed my mind what might have happened if I had still been sitting in the middle – until my grandpa said it. My mom explained that she and I had just switched spots in the car because my brother and I had been arguing. Grandpa told my mom, "You better give thanks to God that she (referring to me) wasn't in the middle because the impact would likely have killed her." When my grandpa got back from collecting our personal items from the car at the wrecking yard, he said that from the looks of the car, it was only by God's grace that any of us in the back seat had survived.

My mom had experienced the worst of that wreck. She suffered a broken neck and was told by doctors that she would never walk again. However, my mom, as stubborn as she was, argued with them and told them that God would heal her. Even though she may not have been "living right" at the time, she still had a strong faith that God would heal her and allow her to walk again. She explained to the doctors that she would walk out of the hospital – and she did – God is good – all the time.

To this day, I sometimes hear my grandpa's words play over in my head like a broken record, "She could be dead." I hate that my mom had to go through that experience, but I do believe God intervened that day, not only for me, but for her as well. He used the accident and her healing for a testimony in her life. Any of us could have died in that back seat. I could be dead, but God spared my life. This is just one more example in my life that God had a specific purpose for me to fulfill. Even though our enemy, the devil, had plans to kill or maim me, God's protection was at work and He causes all things to work together for our good. (Romans 8:28)

And we know that all things work together for good to those who love God, to those who are called according to His purpose.

In the Bible, it tells us that the enemy's objective is to kill and destroy us – thereby destroying our purpose.

The thief does not come except to steal, kill,
and to destroy. I have come that they may have life,
and that they may have it more abundantly.
John 10:10 NKJV

I truly believe that the enemy was attacking me at a very young age to try and stand in the way of me discovering my purpose. Some people would argue and say it was just bad luck or a coincidence. Some might say it's just an accident because accidents happen. But the more you read about my life, the more you will see: it just may be more than that.

I have a purpose!

Chapter 4

Happily Never After

Divorce – (noun) the legal dissolution of a marriage by a court or other competent body; (verb) to legally dissolve one's marriage with someone.

After the accident, my dad came back to live with us and help take care of my mom. Seven months after the accident, in December of 1982, we spent our last Christmas together. In January, 1983, the divorce was final and my dad moved out permanently. The New Year had started out with a terrible bang. I was experiencing the same thing several other kids my age were going through, but the truth was, IT WAS AWFUL! Not only had I lost my daddy, but, because mom had to work tons of hours and sometimes two jobs to pay the bills and keep food on the table, I, essentially, lost my mom, too. I was six years old when I learned what "divorce" was, but it took me years before I understood the impact a divorce can have on all the family members. I have done some research concerning divorce and its effect on the family.

Divorce has a particularly toxic impact on the children involved. According to the U.S. Census Bureau, as of (2017), 19.7 million children (more than one in four) live without a father in the home. Research shows that when a child is raised in a father-absent home, he or she is affected in the following ways:

- Four times greater risk of poverty
- Seven times more likely to become pregnant as a teen
- More likely to have behavioral problems
- More likely to face child abuse and neglect
- Two times greater risk of infant mortality
- More likely to abuse drugs and alcohol
- More likely to go to prison
- Two times more likely to suffer obesity
- More likely to commit a crime
- Two times more likely to drop out of high school

I include this list of statistics to tell you I can personally say that I match five of these characteristics. Between my brothers and I, we have probably met everything on that list.

I do not place blame on anyone for my life. My dad did everything he could to see me, when he was allowed to see me. With all of our moving from town to town because of mom's instability, he tried his best to be a part of my life as often as he could. Sometimes, I do wonder how hard my parents tried to work out their situation and if they had tried harder, how different our lives might have been. I don't regret how we grew up because it made me the person I am today, and I love who I am - now. However, it took years for me to get to this place and to find love for myself. All in all though, I wouldn't change anything.

I included this information for two reasons:

1. I want people to realize how big an impact a father is in their children's lives. If you are reading this and you're a single mom and your ex wants to be a part of their kids' lives, let them! No ifs, ands, or buts about it! Don't punish your kids because of hurts you have toward your ex.

2. Children need both parents. If you are in a troubled relationship, try to be civil and work together for the kid's sake. Let the past go and do your best to get along. Let the other parent be as involved as they want. You are only hurting your kids when you keep them from their other parent. For the betterment of the children, both parents need to be involved in their kid's lives. Let go of pride and selfishness and put your kid's needs first!

Some moms can be bitter because the husband wanted out and then they take it upon themselves to make it impossible for the ex-husband to see the kids. You may have the upper hand because you have custody, but it's not right to use your kids as a bargaining chip against their dad.

When divorced parents can put their personal feelings and emotions aside to get along for the sake of their kids, statistics show that the children have continued stability, close relationships with both parents, and it might make them feel more secure and confident. Children benefit from seeing the parents work together. While the situation may not be ideal and can still be challenging, they can adjust to all the new changes from the divorce a lot easier.

Back to my story:

My mom had to work - a lot. Even though my dad was responsible and paid child support for me, it wasn't enough to help cover bills, groceries and any emergencies that might arise. My two older brothers had a different dad who had given up his parental rights when they were younger so mom was only receiving child support for me. Home life was different, and unstable. We moved around a lot. We lived in some pretty "sketchy" houses and apartments, but I know it's all my mom could afford. I still remember my grandma saying God was always watching over us and she was always praying God's protection over us. I realize now, as an adult, that was her way of saying she was worried about us.

In all the change and adjustments that were going on in our home, my mom had been seeing a man, and it wasn't long before they got married and had my little brother, who is seven years younger than me. Unfortunately, when my brother, Armando, was two weeks old, his father decided he wasn't dad or husband material, so he left my mom for an older woman who didn't have any children. It was his loss because he missed out on one of the coolest, most loving, and full-of-life guys he could have ever had the opportunity to get to know. I love all my brothers. They are all special in their own way. When mom was pregnant with Armando, I always hoped it would be a sister, but when he was born, I didn't love him any less because he was a boy. I loved him instantly and being seven years older, I've always been pretty protective of him. I never got my sister, but God knew what He was doing, and I've been blessed with some pretty amazing sisters-in-law.

My older brothers helped out quite a bit at home since Mom worked a lot. The instability of the home environment and moving around a lot started taking a toll on our education. Moving here and there and switching to different schools so often made it hard on us to learn and make friends. By the age of 16, my oldest brother decided to quit school and get a job to help mom financially. We moved to Fort Worth to start over, and that was even worse. I hated my fourth-grade year in school there. The school was much bigger than where I had come from and the culture was much different. The worst part was that, as the new kid, the other kids were mean to me and I was often bullied.

I didn't want to make much of a fuss about it at home because my mom was stressed out enough, but I truly hated life. We lived in Fort Worth for what seemed (to me) like an eternity, but it was actually less than a year. Then we moved back to Seymour, Texas. However, that didn't last long and by the start of my fifth-grade school year, we were packed up and moving to Sulphur Springs, Texas, where my mom's sister and her husband lived. My mom had heard it was a small town and still believed in the idea of starting over and getting a fresh start somewhere new.

Our first Sunday there, we visited church with my aunt and uncle, and I immediately made a friend. She was sweet and funny and she told me to look for her at recess when I started school. I was already loving this town, especially since I had been dreading having to make new friends. I went to school that following Monday and my friend from church was in my homeroom! I felt lucky because I didn't know if I'd even run into her on that first day. I still think God had a hand in that! The school had only fifth grade classes on this campus, and out of all of the classes, I landed in the one class with my friend from church. They assigned me a seat next to her and she started to show me around school and introduce me to other people. I needed a true friend at that time in my life and it was like she had been hand-picked to be my friend. Out of all the other towns I had lived in, Sulphur Springs, and the people there, were seriously some of the friendliest people I had ever been around.

Besides being the "awkward" years of my life, not much happened or changed between my fifth and seventh grade years. We lived in a lot of different houses in Sulphur Springs, but it was starting to feel like home as we were getting to know more people and get acclimated into the community. A few of mom's other family members started moving to Sulphur Springs, too. It was nice to have some of my many cousins moving closer.

My seventh-grade school year had barely started when mom told us we were moving to Tyler, Texas. This was not exactly the news I wanted to hear. For the first time in my life I had several real friends and I didn't want to move. I even had a "crush" on a boy, but when mom made up her mind, nothing else really mattered. We were moving; it was only a matter of time. I don't recall when we finally moved to Tyler. I was just functioning like a robot. Packing and unpacking started to seem normal in our lives and we were doing it every year – or less. I hated the thought of starting over at a new school, making new friends and all the drama that can come with the middle school years. These years are hard enough for people in stable environments and to have to start from scratch without friends is not a fun beginning.

Tyler was like Fort Worth: culture shock, lots of cliques, and snobby people. I wasn't really bullied as much, and I did make a few friends, but it wasn't much fun being in this big, new town. My new friends all came from wealthier families. They always wanted to go to the mall and shop, or go to the movies, but my mom couldn't afford to give me money to do any of that. They always wanted to do things on weekends while I often had to stay home and babysit my brother so my mom and older brother, Ruben, could work. My brother, Lee, had already moved on and was working and living his own life. I was 13 and my little brother was six. I'm sure mom thought I was the perfect age to be his caretaker so it wouldn't cost her any money.

Tyler was a big change for us. Because money was always so tight, we didn't have cable or much of anything in the way of enter-tainment, so we had to amuse ourselves with board games, reading books, and drawing. I also helped him with homework. When we needed a change of scenery or something different to do, we went to the swimming pool and play area at our apartments. However, we didn't stay outside very long. Since we didn't live in the nicest neighborhoods, we always heard about shootings, stabbings and kidnappings, which made me a little nervous to be out, especially once the sun started going down. I never told my little brother why we had to go inside, and sometimes he got mad because he wanted to swim longer or play with his little friends. I know I was over-protective, but I would demand we go back to the apartment immediately, especially if I got nervous, got a bad feeling about something, or someone stared at one of us for too long.

Even though I wasn't from Tyler, a few of the girls were really nice to me. Sometimes mom would let me spend the night at their houses and attend some slumber parties, but I never felt like I really fit in. Thank God we lived in Tyler for less than a year and then we went back to what always felt like home – good ol' Sulphur Springs, Texas.

By the time we moved back, even my grandparents were settled and living in Sulphur Springs. They had actually been there for a few months, ever since my grandpa had retired from the ministry because he had suffered a few strokes. One of the reasons my mom said we had to move back was so she could help my aunt take care of and check in on my grandparents. But in all reality, I think mom hated Tyler, too. She had been dating a guy from Tyler but then she found out he had been lying to her. He was married. She was, understandably, upset and humiliated, so I know she was also relieved to be back in Sulphur Springs.

Moving back to Sulphur Springs was a huge blessing. My grandparents had always been our safety net, and it was good to be back close to them. It was also nice to have adults to hang out with when mom was always working. My brother, Ruben, was married now and was living his own life, too.

After being back in Sulphur Springs for a few months, my mom started dating someone, which eventually led to another marriage. I didn't care for the man, not because he wasn't my dad, but because he wasn't what he presented himself to be to every-one else. He fought with my mom over the stupidest things and even sought out fights with me and my little brother. It was like having another child in the house rather than having another adult. He lied to my mom all the time and even when she caught him in his lies, she stayed with him. I know she just wanted a marriage to work, but she was experiencing failed marriages and relation-ships one right after the other. I was annoyed that my mom put up with the behavior of this man, so I started to act out and get a little disrespectful with her. I was young and immature, and definitely did not handle things correctly, but I also began to be rebellious against her. Subconsciously, I chose to rebel because I had lost a lot of respect for my mom over the years, especially with the way this man treated her. I am sure for her it was a relief not to have to work two jobs just to make ends meet, but she sacrificed so much more in staying in this relationship.

Now, I'm not condoning my behavior at all. I'm just telling my story and how I acted. I believe we should do as the Bible says and always honor our parents, even if – from our perspective – they are wrong or make decisions we don't agree with. It's easy to say that, now that I am a parent. One of my biggest regrets is how I didn't respect my parents during those times. I began lying to my mom. I became resentful, hateful, and bitter about what we were going through and what we didn't have. I truly lost sight of who I was.

My mom would threaten to send me to live with my dad or that she would tell my dad. One thing about my dad, he expected me to respect adults – even my mom's new husband – regardless of how I felt about him. At the time, I wasn't the least bit worried. My thoughts were: at least I won't have to live here with this man, mom's husband, who was a total jerk to her, to me, and my little brother. He and I rarely exchanged words or even looked at each other. He knew I didn't like him, and I think he felt the same about me since I wasn't the easiest teenager to live with. Looking back now, I do hate that. I should have been more respectful, regardless of how I felt about him.

My grandma didn't want me to leave to go live in Wichita Falls. She liked having us nearby. She suggested to my mom that I come live with them because I wouldn't treat them badly, and she was right. I never would have done anything to hurt or disrespect my grandparents. However, this arrangement didn't last but a few months because my aunts and uncles didn't like the idea of me living there. They thought a teenager living with my grandparents, at their age, was too much for them to handle. It was great while it lasted but, unfortunately, my time with them quickly came to an end.

The only thought I had in my mind was that I was not going back to live with my mom and her husband. I didn't actually *hate* him, but I certainly didn't like being around him or the fighting that occurred at home. My older brothers liked him, or at least tolerated him, but they didn't have to live with him. My little brother seemed okay with him, but I really couldn't make myself like him. I would hear him tell stories and I would roll my eyes because I could see right through his over-exaggerated stories and lies.

My mom finally made the call to my dad and off I went to Wichita Falls at the beginning of my eighth-grade year. I did not live with my dad though because he and my mom agreed that I still needed to be around a woman and have a motherly-like figure in my life. Dad wasn't married so my older cousin and her husband graciously opened their home to me. I attended the best junior high school in Wichita Falls and I actually had my own room, my own television, and I had a bed that was covered with girly bedding. I even had my own phone! It was heaven on earth compared to the last seven years since the divorce. I had been sharing a room with my mom or with my little brother so finally having my own things was a big deal to me. I never realized it until the day I moved in and thought, "Wow! This is what I've been missing out on!" I can't put on paper how special I felt in that moment. It wasn't that I was materialistic or anything like that. I had just never understood what it was like to have my very own things.

I am not complaining about the situation I had grown up in or how we lived. I think Mom tried her best, but it's all she could afford. I always had a bed to sleep on, regardless of whether I shared it with someone else. We had to share everything. I never had a girly-room with decorations. I was always too embarrassed to have friends over just to hang out. I also never asked anyone to spend the night because I had to share a room with my little brother. So, it was a big deal for me to be able to have a room of my own.

I had other cousins my age who lived in Wichita Falls so it was nice to already have friends when I started at the new school. Knowing that I was related to them made it easier to make friends and it was great. I lived in Wichita Falls for my eighth and ninth grade school years. Even though it was nice to have cousins my age to hang out with, I did make some new friends. Some of those friends were a lot more materialistically and sexually advanced than what I had been around in Sulphur Springs. Many of these new friends came from money so it was easier to get alcohol and drugs. It was a whole new world. The peer pressure was real. I was introduced to a teen club, which is where we went on weekends to hang out. Of course, they could not serve alcohol but I had friends who had easy access to it. It was easy to leave, have some drinks and come back and dance with your friends. I was really trying my best to fit in with this new crowd.

The summer before my freshman year, one of my new friends, Amy, began dating a guy named Jimmy. He was a little older than us, and he had a driver's license. His parents always seemed to be out of town. One Friday night when she was spending the night at my house, we had made plans to go to the mall, hang out at the arcade (where we usually ran into all of our school friends), and then go to a movie. However, not long after we were dropped off at the mall, Jimmy showed up and asked her to come with him to his house. She didn't want to leave me there since she was staying with me and I guess his plans were for them to be alone because he wasn't too thrilled that I was coming along. After all, in most instances, three is a crowd. When we got to his house, we were all sitting in the living room watching MTV and he kept whispering to her. They were giggling and talking when suddenly someone knocked on the door. It was two guys and three girls who were his friends from a different school.

They proceeded to get into Jimmy's dad's liquor cabinet and started drinking. They offered us some, but I was afraid we would get busted and I was already nervous about not being at the mall. If someone saw us leave with that guy, I knew I would be grounded for a long time. Amy didn't drink either. Evidently, Jimmy's friends knew his parents were always out of town and before long, a few more guys and girls around our age had arrived. It was turning into a party. To my surprise, this didn't sit well with Amy's boyfriend. He grabbed Amy and took her toward his parent's bedroom. As she left the room, she looked at me with a desperate look on her face and waved for me to follow them. I didn't know if she was scared he would try to do take advantage of her but I did what any good friend would do. I followed her. A few other people actually followed behind me and when we got into the room there was a total of about six of us. I vividly remember standing there in front of Jimmy and Amy as they sat on the bed. I was looking at her, trying to ask her with my eyes yet without saying a word, why she had wanted me to follow her into his parents' bedroom. Less than a minute went by when out of nowhere, Jimmy totally lost it. He reached into his parent's nightstand and pulled out a gun.

I wanted to disappear – and quick. He was waving it around franticly and cussing at everyone, telling them they needed to leave. He didn't want people messing up the house because his parents were due back the next day and he didn't want all of these people trashing his house. In that moment, it was like he completely lost his mind. Before this, I thought Jimmy had seemed so nice. He was attractive, and popular. Now I saw him as a maniac. I remember seeing the gun pointing in my direction as he waved it. He wasn't specifically pointing it at me. I was just the one closest to them. Talk about being at the wrong place at the wrong time! I immediately began praying in my head. I asked God to save us and to forgive me for being disobedient and leaving the mall when I knew I shouldn't have. I was repenting and asking God to forgive all my wrongs. I hoped that, if something happened to me, my family knew how much I loved them. I kept replaying all of the events of that day and how this night could have gone so much differently if I had only put my foot down and told Amy we couldn't leave with Jimmy.

Everyone left quickly and he finally calmed down. He put the gun away and Amy asked him to please take us back to the mall. She played it off that she didn't want me to get in trouble since she was spending the night with me. The ride back to the mall was quiet and somber. They didn't speak to each other the entire car ride and she didn't even kiss him goodnight. She said bye, got out of the car, waved at him, and we walked back into the mall.

A few weeks later, we found out that he was on medication for some mental issues. He couldn't keep a girlfriend because he always did crazy things and blew up in a rage, like he had that night. I replayed that moment in my head for months, thinking how that night could have ended so differently. I can still see it in slow motion – like a suspenseful movie. Being on the other end of that gun and watching it wave in front of my face, seeing him lose his temper, acting irrationally and thinking, "Lord, please don't let this be the end of life for me." He could have shot one or two of us, or all of us, or even himself. I truly believe God was watching over me that night. This is just another example to show that God is so good!

I have a purpose!

Chapter 5

He is our Life Giver

Toward the end of my freshman year, my grandpa fell ill and was in and out of the hospital a lot. My dad drove me from Wichita Falls to Sulphur Springs to see him one weekend because the doctors told our family that he really didn't have much time left. I was able to spend time with him and tell him how much I loved him. A few short weeks later, my grandpa went to be with the Lord.

It was a very heartbreaking day. Even though he had 49 grandchildren, I know I was his favorite granddaughter. It wasn't a secret and my mom would often remind me of how close I was to him. I know a lot of my cousins hated that and were jealous of our relationship, but what they didn't understand is that we stayed with my grandparents a lot and even had to live with them off and on. Our grandparents filled that parental role that we missed and needed daily. My brothers and I got to bond and spend more time with them than most of their other grandchildren. As a grandparent now, I know that they didn't love us more, or think that we were more special than the rest of their grandkids. They were just doing what they needed to. It's what any grandparent would do.

On the day we buried my grandpa, some of my favorite memories flashed in my mind and warmed my heart. I remembered when he would pick me up from grade school in Seymour and take me out for ice cream or some afternoon snack. Sometimes we would go to a little store and he gave me money to buy something, not because I asked for anything but just because he wanted to spoil me.

There were some Saturday mornings when my mom had to work and we would get to tag along to garage sales with him and my grandma. He was always so joyful and full of life. I loved that man so much. He would crack jokes that would make my brothers and me laugh. My grandma would just roll her eyes as I'm sure she had heard those jokes a thousand times, which made us all laugh even more. He would watch wrestling with us and tell us how fake it was, but we all enjoyed it together. Anytime we had any little cough or cold or stomachache he would pray over us. They didn't believe in running to the doctor for every little thing – they believed in prayer and God's healing power.

As they started lowering the casket into the ground, I finally snapped out of my memories and continued watching, my dad on one side of me and my brother, Ruben, on the other. Watching all of his children and grandchildren with sadness and tears in their eyes, the emotions were overwhelming. It was amazing to see all the people who showed up for his service. Some of his previous church members and other pastors and preachers from other towns were present. It was a huge turnout. He had made an impact on so many lives and was loved by many.

This all took place the summer before my sophomore year. My mom took her father's passing hard. She asked me to come back and live with them. Even though she was still married to the man that I didn't care for, somehow, I felt like she needed me. Honestly, I thought it would be best for me because I was making some bad choices in Wichita Falls. I decided I would move back to live with mom and her husband, and my little brother, who now lived in Floresville, Texas, a small town about 30 miles from San Antonio, Texas.

I felt like this was a good move. It was summertime, I was learning how to drive, and I got involved in the church they were attending. I made friends and attended a lot of youth-related church services. I felt like I was getting myself together in a good way. I started my sophomore year at school in Floresville, but less than six weeks later, we moved again. This time, it was to a smaller town called Poth, which worked out nicely because most of the kids who attended school there went to the same church we attended. I even knew and recognized a lot of the teachers. Mom and her husband started having problems, so they moved to Austin for a job for him, but I chose to stay in Poth with my oldest brother, Lee, until the semester was over. By the time the semester was over, mom was already living back in Sulphur Springs.

I was glad to be moving back to Sulphur Springs, where it had always felt like home. I had written and stayed in contact with several of my friends from middle school there, so I was able to pick up where I left off. It was nice to be able to see them in person. It was as if I had never left. I soon became friends with a new girl that had just moved to town. She wasn't from Sulphur Springs, but we had classes together, and she was a lot of fun. Nora was old enough to drive and came from a broken home, too. Because we had a lot in common, we got along really well.

Nora was a little older than me and had a lot of older friends, so we acted older when we were around them. We would ride around on the weekends and stop to talk to them. One night, we met up with a guy named Rob, who I found out was a year older than us and one of her beer suppliers. She sometimes got beer from Rob and then we would go hang out and drink – either at some of our friend's houses, in pastures, or at parties. I was being stupid and trying to fit in, but inside I felt so much conviction. I knew right from wrong, but when you're 15, everything inside you just wants to be cool, so you take part in activities to be like everyone else.

The weekend partying went on throughout my sophomore year. I didn't really have any serious boyfriends that year, although I had some dates and actually dated one guy for a few months. Still, I hadn't seriously fallen for anyone. At the time, I had no idea that I had already met the love of my life.

Nora started dating a guy and had less time for me, which was okay. I started hanging out with another girl who ended up being a lifetime bestie, Misty. She and I were inseparable. We had classes together, did school projects together, and I spent a lot of time at her house. The atmosphere at her house was always welcoming. Her parents were always so sweet! I'm glad they didn't get tired of seeing me over there every day!

Misty told me that the beer supplier, Rob, had been her boy-friend her freshman year, but it was one of those relationships that consisted of just talking on the phone. They didn't get to go on dates because neither of them could drive and they weren't old enough to really go out when they dated. Nevertheless, she still had a "crush" on him. I figured she and Rob would eventually get back together. I didn't know Rob or anything about him, except for what she told me, but I encouraged her that if she liked him, she should tell one of his friends.

Girls aren't usually bold enough to just come out and tell a guy they like him, but one thing that always seemed to work is to tell their friends. The information would usually get back to your "crush" pretty quickly. It's funny how guys say girls can't keep a secret, but I think they are just as bad!

One Friday night, Misty, Nora, a few friends and I had planned a girls night out. Misty showed up early to get ready at my house and she told me she had talked to Rob. I was excited for her! I asked her if she told him or his best friend and she said no. She said he only wanted to talk to her about me. I was confused because we didn't know each other. Rob had asked Misty if he asked me out if she thought I would say yes. I was shocked. I told her I wouldn't go out with him; I wouldn't do that to her.

I had never even spoken to Rob except one time when we rode around with Nora and one of his friends. She had been drinking and couldn't drive, so he and I sat in the front seat together driving her car around until she sobered up a bit. The only conversation I really had with him was to give him directions back to Sulphur Springs. We had been driving around on back roads and he managed to get so turned around and lost, he couldn't find his way back. I'm pretty sure that was all we talked about, but I guess I made an impression.

After a long and private conversation between Misty and me, she talked me into giving Rob a chance if he asked me out on a date. I didn't want to if she still had feelings for him, but she shared with me that, since our previous conversation about Rob, she had actually started talking to someone else in the last few days.

Even with her permission, I wasn't sure I'd say yes. I didn't really know him, I was super shy and the whole dating thing terrified me. I didn't like the idea of dates because it meant eating, and I didn't want to eat in front of a guy. I know it's stupid, but I didn't really know how to act around guys. I didn't have older sisters and you just don't ask your mom for dating tips!

I was worried about being hurt if I ended up falling for a guy only to realize that he didn't like me. I was very good at putting up walls and keeping my distance from people for fear of getting hurt. You have to understand – when kids or teenagers come from broken homes – it's hard for them to imagine themselves in healthy relationships. It's easier to imagine yourself as undeserving and not even attempt a relationship because you're already carrying so much baggage from growing up around unhealthy and broken relationships.

We continued to get ready for our night out and Misty said, "Just in case we run into Rob tonight when we're out riding around, should I tell him that you would say yes if he asked you out?" I told her I didn't know. I was hesitant because I didn't know what he was like and didn't know anything about him. She said, "I'm going to tell him to go ahead and ask you out and you better say yes." She told me how nice he was, that he would be sweet to me, and that I should give him a chance. I finally agreed that I would say yes and at least go out with him once. The more I thought about it, I felt like one date couldn't hurt.

The opportunity came sooner than I expected. We all went out, ate, and rode around. Then we decided that, since my mom was out of town, we would go back to my place and drink and stay in. However, the news that we were going to be drinking traveled fast, and several other girls and guys showed up to party, including Rob. That night, we must have gotten a little rowdy because the cops showed up and the party ended pretty fast. As soon as he saw them show up, Rob ran to the kitchen and hid all the beer and alcohol. There were so many people at the house for the cops to check, it bought him some time. Thanks to Rob's quick and sneaky thinking, none of us were given "minor-in-possession" violations. They may have known we had it, but because they couldn't find any alcohol, they couldn't issue us tickets. That was really lucky, too, because I was afraid of what would happen if I got a ticket. The wrath of my mom would not have been good.

The only four people who stayed to help me clean up the mess left from the party were my best friend Misty, my best guy friend, Dave, Nora's boyfriend, Andy, and Rob. Nora's mom had made her leave earlier and I was told that she and I couldn't be friends any-more. The funny thing was – and what Nora's mom didn't know – was that Nora had been more of a bad influence on me than I had been on her. She was the one with all the connections to people who could supply us beer and wine coolers, but I didn't want to tell her mom. With the crowd gone and after the cleaning was completed, Rob and I stood outside talking and he finally asked me to go out on a date with him. After all the goings-on and activities of the night, I felt like we had already known each other forever. He was extremely helpful and sweet, so without hesitation, I said yes.

The following Friday night, we went out on a date and he was the perfect gentleman. I was impressed at how relaxed I was around him. I even ate in front of him! We had a good time and got to know each other better. One date led to another, and we started spending more time together. The guy Misty had been talking to didn't work out, so she was always with me. We were kind of a package deal, so Misty came with us on most of our dates, but Rob never seemed to care. We always had fun and lots of laughs. Things started getting serious, and he finally asked me to be his girlfriend and to wear his class ring. Here I was, dating the love of my life at 16 years old and didn't even have a clue that he would be more than just another "crush."

I was definitely smitten and pretty sure I loved him. I couldn't imagine going even one day without seeing or talking to him. He had already become, not just my boyfriend, but my best friend. I told him everything. I even talked to him about my home life and all of the mess I had gone through, so much of which is not even mentioned in this book. I didn't hold anything back from Rob. He knew everything about me and still stuck around, which to me was priceless. I felt like I had finally found someone with whom I could be totally real! I didn't have to pretend to be someone I wasn't, be ashamed of who I was or embarrassed by my upbringing. He loved me for everything I was and everything I wasn't. He knew more things about me than I had ever shared with my best girl friends or even any of my ex-boyfriends.

One fall morning in October of my junior year of high school, I woke up running a high fever and vomiting. I had chills, was really dizzy, and I had an excruciating headache that felt like someone had hit me with a baseball bat. Since I had always been a healthy kid and never had to see any doctors, I didn't have a regular doctor. The clinic in town wouldn't see me as a new patient and they couldn't work me in that day, so my mom had to take me to my little brother's pediatrician.

Because this was before every teenager had a cell phone (which we, surprisingly, survived without), I couldn't let Rob know I wouldn't be at school. He had to be at school really early for "zero hour" and I went to classes later than he did. It made me sad when I imagined his face that morning. He would always walk out to my car to meet me so he could walk me into school, but today, I wouldn't be there. I wondered what he would be thinking when I didn't show up. I wondered if he would miss me, or just go on about his day. I was thinking all these thoughts as I laid my head on my mom's lap in the doctor's office.

There I was, a 16-year-old teenager in a kid clinic. I was watching the doctor as he came out in the lobby area sticking suckers in the kid's mouths. When he got in front of us and saw me, he said, "She's sick, momma." I thought, "Duh! Why else would I be here?"

He offered me a sucker and I barely muttered out a "No, thank you." My head was pounding and the light in the room was so bright it was making me even more nauseous. They finally got me back into one of the rooms and he concluded that, based on my symptoms, it was the flu. He didn't test me for anything, but it was the beginning of flu season so it made sense to us. He sent me home with instructions to rest, drink lots of fluids, and take the medicines he was prescribing.

When we arrived back home, I went straight to sleep on the couch. My mom didn't want to leave me alone. She was pretty worried about me because I was really weak, could barely make it to the bathroom on my own, and the vomiting still hadn't subsided. Since Rob went to school earlier in the day, he usually got out of school early as well. As soon as he could, he came straight to my house to check on me. My mom told him what the doctor had said and asked him if he could stay with me while she went to pick up my medicines, stop to buy me fluids and soups, and pick up my little brother from school. He agreed to stay and take care of me while she went to run those errands. I barely remember much after that. I know mom came home and Rob stayed for a while, but I had slept the whole time he had been there. I didn't have the energy to talk. I remember him telling me he loved me, saying goodbye, and kissing me on the forehead when he left. I honestly don't know how I made it from the living room couch to my bed, but I woke up the next morning in my bed.

The next morning, we realized my condition had worsened. I had tried to shower but fell in the shower because I was dizzy and seeing colored spots. I had never been that sick in my life. My mom had not been able to get the fever to break and now the fever was even higher than the day before. My mom's "mother's intuition" knew something just didn't feel right. She made me get dressed so she could take me back to the doctor. I didn't want to because I didn't have the energy to move, but I knew it wouldn't do any good to argue with her.

Shortly after we arrived at the same doctor's office, they got me right back to a room. The concerned doctor informed my mom that I had lost 13 pounds from the day before. I was dehydrated, and my fever was dangerously high. He said, "I'm sending her to the hospital for a spinal tap and more testing." As soon as we arrived at the hospital, they immediately started testing me. They did blood work and tried to administer an IV but, because of the dehydration from all the vomiting, they couldn't find a vein to work. My arms looked like a pin cushion from all the attempts to find a vein. My mom called the high school and left a message for Rob that I was in the hospital and she asked him to come by when he got out of school. He showed up and waited with mom as they watched the nurses and doctors frantically try to get my fever down. I only remember bits and pieces from that day but I do remember it made me nervous to see the concern on everyone's faces. The spinal tap results finally came in. I had tested positive for meningococcal meningitis.

My doctor told my mom they would have to send me immediately to Children's Medical Hospital in Dallas by Care Flight. He also told my mom to love on me and tell me goodbye because he couldn't guarantee that I would make it to the hospital. I was in very grave condition. She couldn't fly with me; she would have to drive to Dallas. They also told her they didn't know if I would make it through the night.

My mom did come kiss me and tell me she loved me, but she didn't say goodbye. She said, "I will be calling your aunts and uncles and we will be putting you on their church prayer list. I will be at the hospital in a few hours." She reminded me that we believe in a God who heals and that I was going to pull out of this. I could hear everything she told me; I just didn't have the strength to reply. Rob came over and kissed me and told me he loved me before they loaded me onto the helicopter. I remember thinking, "I've never flown. This is going to be my first experience of getting to fly and it's on a helicopter." They had me on a stretcher and loaded me into the helicopter. I remember looking out of the window and watching my mom and Rob stand there until we had gotten far enough that I couldn't see them anymore. I found out later that they stood out there and watched until they could no longer see the helicopter. I did wish at that moment that I would have had the strength to tell them I loved them too, but I couldn't talk much. I just replied by looking or shaking my head. I had just been told I was dying and I was trying to wrap my befuddled mind around those words. I remember feeling so weak. I would open my eyes and listen for a few minutes, then shut them again. It even hurt to keep my eyes open. The emergency services attendant on the care flight was very attentive and sweet, talked to me the whole time, held my hand, and explained what all the noises and beeping was around me. I don't remember speaking at all while I was in there, but I remember it appeared to be a really quick trip. It seemed like we had just left, then suddenly we had landed, and they were unloading me out of the helicopter and taking me to ICU.

They had a whole team of doctors and an outstanding nursing staff waiting for me to arrive. My ICU room was full of windows and it faced the nurse's station. I didn't like it, but it made me realize the severity of the situation. I found out meningitis was highly contagious so all the nurses, doctors and anyone who came in the room had to wear a gown, a face mask, shoe coverings, and something over their head. It was weird seeing every visitor or hospital staff put on all that garb before they could enter my room. My mom finally arrived, and even though she knew it was highly contagious, as soon as she arrived she came in and kissed me, with her doctor-ordered mask on, of course. By the time I went to sleep that night, they had managed to get my fever to come down and the vomiting/dry heaves had finally stopped. I was actually a little hungry and asking for Jell-O since I hadn't been able to keep anything down in two days. I was in ICU for a few days and then they moved me to a private room where I would be able to have visitors. Up until this point, the only one allowed in the room was my mom and the hospital staff.

Once I got settled in my private room, I was told that my dad and some other family members were on their way to see me. Rob called to say he was coming to see me, too.

After my dad arrived, the doctors spoke to him and my mom and informed them that with meningitis there might be some long-term problems that could stay or arise later, and some effects could become permanent from having had meningitis. A few of the possible problems they described were: permanent brain damage, partial or total hearing loss, some paralysis, intellectual disabilities, behavioral problems, personality changes, or even heart or liver problems. My mom, knowing the power of prayer and what God had done in our lives in the past, told them this situation wouldn't be any different than any we had faced before. She told the doctors, "We believe in a God who heals. Thank you for the information and concern but I don't believe my daughter will have any problems. When the time comes for her to walk out the doors, she will be completely healed!"

Every day, I started to feel better. I was asking for food, coloring books, colors, and puzzles. Because I was in a children's hospital, they didn't have a lot to entertain a 16-year old girl, besides a VCR and movies, and I was tired of watching TV. They brought in several specialists and doctors to run multiple tests to see if I was making progress. My team of doctors were amazed at how well I was doing in such a short amount of time. I felt well enough to go home and kept asking the staff about it, but I had to pass all the tests before they would even consider the thought of releasing me.

On my eighth day there, one of my doctor's told mom that I would be able to leave the next day after some hearing tests. They were amazed at how fast I had recovered. They said it usually took 14 to 21 days for a full recovery or, in the most severe cases, people my age usually died from being that sick with meningitis. My mom knew it was God who had healed me; there was no doubt in her mind. I also give credit to the amazing doctors and nurses at Children's Medical Hospital of Dallas, who took very good care of me.

The day finally arrived for me to be dismissed. The ride home seemed very long. I was tired of sitting since that was what I had been doing for several days. Dallas is 80 miles west of where I lived, and the trip gave me some time to think. I kept replaying in my head the words of the doctor before they put me on the helicopter, "Momma, tell her goodbye; she might not make it through the night." Then I remembered hearing my grandpa say, "She could have died in that car wreck." The memory of the gun incident from my freshman year came back to my mind as well, watching that gun wave in front of me and thinking that my time was up.

I couldn't shake these memories. They kept playing like a broken record stuck on repeat. All I could say to myself at the time was, "Thank God I'm still alive." I was so happy and overwhelmed with joy because I was well, and I was alive.

I have a purpose!

But indeed, for this very reason I have allowed you to live, in order to show you my power and in order that my name be proclaimed throughout the Earth.
Exodus 9:16

Chapter 6
Life after Death

It's obvious that I didn't die, but having come close, I felt like I had a new perspective on life – I guess as much as any normal 16-year-old would have. However, it didn't take long before I was back to my same routine of going to school and working part time. Any free time I did get, I wanted to spend it with Rob.

A few months went by and my mom got the urge to move again, but this time I was putting up a fight. I didn't want to leave! I was a junior in high school, and I wanted to finish school in Sulphur Springs. I was in love and I didn't want to leave Rob. He didn't want me to leave either and told me if I had to move, he would follow me wherever we went and just get a job and live on his own. Rob's mom came to the rescue. He had already warned her that if I had to move and leave town, he was moving too. His mom knew he was serious and didn't want her son leaving home, so she went to talk to my mom. Rob's mom told my mom that she had a house big enough for me to live with them and that I would have my own room. My mom had a few requests and his mom agreed to them. It was a done deal; I would get to move in with Rob when my mom moved. This arrangement wasn't the best idea, but I'm sure our moms trusted us and hoped we could keep our hands off each other. I did have my own room, and we were supposed to sleep in our own rooms, but the truth is that it didn't take long for us to start living like a married couple, in every sense of the term. His mom was gone a lot and I don't know whether she was naïve or just trusted we would do the right thing, but after all, we were teenagers with hormones. It wasn't a wise decision to leave us alone. All had been great in our relationship – prior to living together.

After a while, I think all the togetherness at school and at home was starting to get to us. After living with him for about four months, our relationship suddenly went from dating to moving way too fast. We started arguing a lot and we found out really quickly how much we could get on each other's nerves. We started finding less time for each other and trying to make more time for our friends. We broke up a few times, but by the end of the day we would get back together. This went on for a few weeks until one rainy, dreary, Saturday morning in late April. This particular day, we were both off work, which rarely happened. It was going to be a good day to be lazy, and although we were both hungry, we dreaded getting out of the house at all. I decided to go get us some food. When I returned, there wasn't any sign of Rob – just a note left on my pillow. He did what we both had been wanting to do for weeks. In the note, he told me the arguing and not getting along had gotten to be too much and he was tired of it. He talked about how our relationship had gotten too serious too quickly and he thought we needed to give each other some space. He told me he loved me, and it hurt him to do this, but felt that we both needed a break from each other. In my head, I knew everything he was saying was right. He also said that he hoped we could be friends eventually and that if I wanted to, I could still live there. He just felt as though, at least for now, we would just get along better as friends only. He reminded me that I did have my own room and that we could be grown up and just be friends so that I could still have a place to live.

To say that I was upset was an understatement! Really? A note was all I got? Rage flew all over me! We had dated for ten months and he broke up with me in a note! Couldn't he at least have the courtesy to tell me in person? I was mad and hurt but also relieved that he had been mature enough to "rip the band-aid off." We both knew it was coming, but up until that day, neither one of us had the courage to do it. I immediately started packing my personal property. This was one thing I was good at and had plenty of experience doing. At my age, I could have already been a professional packer and mover.

There was no way in the world I was going to stay living under the same roof with someone who just broke my heart! While I packed, I was trying to keep my emotions under control but the more I packed, the angrier I got. I started loading up my car and then the thought crossed my mind: Where was I going? I had been so consumed by packing, anger, and sadness that I hadn't considered where I was going to live. Where was I supposed to go? We had never thought of a backup plan in case this arrangement went south. Mom was living in Austin again, but I did have uncles and aunts in Sulphur Springs, and my grandma. I decided to go to my mom's sister's house. My aunt was always a good listener. I told her what had happened and explained that I really didn't want to call my mom because she would want me to move to Austin. My aunt explained that I would have to tell my mom but that I was welcome to stay with them for a while if I needed to, at least until the end of the school year since we only had about seven weeks left until summer break. I decided to spend the night there, but I still had to go get the rest of my things from Rob's house.

I had been living with him for several months now but had never much paid attention to this little bridge by his house. On this particularly gloomy, still rainy Saturday, that bridge grabbed my attention as I drove over it. Something about it felt like it was calling my name. Thinking about it now, that small bridge was almost eerie, yet enticing that day. It really had my attention.

I arrived at Rob's and walked right in to grab the rest of my clothes and possessions. Sadness and bitterness was setting in – even worse than earlier in the day when I had left with the first load. After finally getting all my things, I quickly went back to my car. I was grateful he hadn't come back yet to see me leaving because I didn't want him to see me hurting. I was trying to be tough, but on the inside, I felt as though my world was crashing in and I was dying. As my thoughts were spinning circles in my head, a stupidly evil thought crossed my mind.

After I left Rob's house and right before I got close to the bridge, I thought, "I'll just kill myself. I'll drive off this bridge and either hurt myself in a bad way or kill myself." Now 28 years later, I know it was just the enemy trying to get me to end my life. I wasn't then, nor have I ever been depressed, and I wasn't suicidal. I was just being stupid and listening to the wrong voices that day. I thought it would serve him right to have to live with the guilt of hurting me enough emotionally to the point where I took my life.

I knew how stupid and immature that was the minute I tried it. It had still been raining a hard-steady rain. Without hesitation or fear, I jerked my steering wheel to try and force myself over the bridge, but my car didn't do what I thought or had imagined. To this very day, I am positive that God took control of my car. The minute I tried to make my car spin off of the bridge, an unexplainable force pulled my steering wheel and jolted me back into my lane. It was as if Someone had literally picked my car up and put it back in my lane. At first, I thought, "What in the heck was that?" Then I thought to myself, "You idiot! Just six months ago you were asking God to spare your life as you were dying from meningitis and this is how you show Him you appreciate the life He gave you?" I started crying and had to pull over at the nearest convenience store on my way to my aunt's house to compose myself. I know with everything inside me and beyond the shadow of a doubt, God intervened that day. It's a wonder there were no other cars coming towards me on that busy highway. A few other scenarios have gone through my mind since that day, but God is good and always faithful.

I Have a Purpose!

I did ask God to forgive me. I didn't want to be ungrateful for the life He had given me. I stayed with my aunt for a few nights and then decided to find somewhere else to stay. I loved my aunt and uncle and was very grateful for the hospitality, but the rules were way too strict and seemed a little extreme for me, especially since I had already tasted the freedom of being without parents.

Off I went again. This time I headed over to see my Uncle Roy, mom's brother. He and mom had always been pretty close siblings and they always helped each other out, so I dropped by his house. No sooner had I gotten out of the car and started on the spiel I had been rehearsing in my mind when he said, "Mija." (In Spanish, that means "my daughter" but we Hispanics use this word like we use "sweetie" or "honey" in East Texas.)

He said, "Mija, do you need a place to stay?" I shook my head yes with the biggest lump in my throat. I didn't really want to have to say any more than that because I knew I'd lose my composure and fall apart. It had been the worst few days of my life and I was an emotional wreck, so I'm glad he didn't let me give the whole sob story I had prepared. It may have been rehearsed in my mind, but it was all the truth. My life was a mess! He told me his house was my house and I was welcome to stay as long as I needed. He immediately pulled a house key off his key chain and handed it to me, then told me to pop the trunk so he could help me unload my belongings. He said the only thing I had to do while I was there was pick up after myself and do my own laundry so his wife wouldn't have to do it. He said if I was going to be out late to let them know so they wouldn't worry about me and that, on occasion, they would need me to help out by taking his kids to school on my way to school. All that seemed more than fair to me. He handed me a $20 bill and said if I needed anything to let him know. I didn't want to take his money since he was providing me with a roof over my head, but he insisted. He told me to take it for gas money, or a burger, or whatever. My uncle was always a generous man.

All was good at my uncle's house until about three or four weeks later. One evening when I was out with my friends, partying again, I suddenly started to feel ill. This had never happened before. I had gotten drunk several times and I was never one to throw up or have a hangover. Several of my guy friends always teased me saying I was the only girl they knew that could out drink them and still function the next day. I'm not bragging, and it's not anything I'm proud of. If anything, it's quite the opposite. I'm just making the point that this particular night, I was super sick, despite the fact I had barely been drinking at all! It was like nothing I had ever experienced, and it made no sense at all. I had felt fine all day until I started drinking. Even then, I was not throwing up, just very nauseated, having major cramps, and an excruciating pain in my stomach and back. It was a pain I had never experienced before. I was starting to worry a little. Although I had been drinking, I knew who God was and how much He could do for me. With the worry and pain I was feeling, I started praying in my mind. I knew whatever it was, God could make the pains go away and heal me. I had already told my uncle I was staying the night with my friend, so I confided in her and told her I was sick and something wasn't right. Something inside me told me to stop drinking that night because it was making the pain in my stomach worse. I called it quits that night earlier than usual and we headed back to my friend's house. As she and I talked while we were getting ready for bed, she asked if there was any way I could be pregnant. Oh, my goodness!! I sat up in the bed and said, "I don't think so," but my mind began to wander. As I thought about my menstrual cycle, I remembered that the last two months hadn't been "normal," but surely it couldn't be that! I thought to myself, "Isn't this just great! The last time I talked to Rob's best friend, he told me Rob was signing up to join the Air Force." I wondered if he would even want to know if I happened to be pregnant. So many thoughts and questions swirled through my mind. Needless to say, I barely slept a wink that night. I prayed to God that if I was pregnant that my baby would be okay. I asked God to forgive me. I felt so bad that I had been drinking and could have harmed the little human that might be inside of me. I knew what I had to do... I needed to find out for sure if I was pregnant.

The very next Monday, my best guy friend, Dave, convinced me to go to the doctor to get tested. I had confided in him because, besides Misty, he was the closest person I had at the time. I had family, but I couldn't tell them that I could be pregnant. I decided to go to Dave's mom's doctor because I was afraid my mom's doctor or nurse would tell my mom. I was young and didn't know a lot, but I also didn't want a lot of people knowing my business, especially since I was still trying to figure out what in the world was going on in my life. I didn't need a lot of opinions and uninvited advice.

At the doctor's office, I had barely left the restroom where I had left the cup for the nurse to test and hadn't even had a chance to sit back down in the waiting room when the nurse said, "Melissa, come here please." I went back to the hallway and she said she had barely put the test strip in when it already had a strong positive. She wanted to know when my last real period was. After I told her, she said, "Based on that information, sweetie, you're right around 3 months pregnant – give or take a few days." This made so much sense now! The mood swings, the emotional episodes... I was also sure that was why I had felt so sick when I drank a few nights ago. I was so immature and young! How was I supposed to be a mom? I knew one thing for sure – I wasn't going to drink again, especially now that I knew I was going to be a mother. I needed to straighten myself out. My first reaction was shock and fear, and tears of course, because I felt so alone. I wondered how I was supposed to be a mom and take care of another human – since I wasn't doing a very good job of taking care of myself!

I confided to a few of my close friends that I was pregnant, but they were sworn to secrecy. My mom had come back to town to visit and told me she thought she was moving back to Sulphur Springs, which meant I was going to have to tell her. I waited till she had found a place to live and had moved in before I told her. There was not much I could hide from my mom. My mom has that same thing her dad always had – anytime you were going to tell her something, she usually already knew because God had already prepared her.

I went to her apartment to tell her but didn't go inside. I stood in the doorway and said, "Mom, I need to tell you something." When she said, "I know," I started thinking, "Which one of my big mouth friends told her?" I asked her what she knew. She said, "I know you have something important to tell me and that I need to hear you out and be here for you." She also told me she wasn't going to be mad. Sometimes, my mom was scary. She may look nice and sweet, but something about that 5-foot woman always terrified me. I finally told her I was well over 3 months pregnant and that Rob was the dad. I also told her that even though we had promised both her and his mom that we wouldn't, we had been having sex for a while. She wasn't mad like I thought she would be. She said I needed to tell him and his mom and that she would go with me if I needed her to. I opted to go with a friend instead. I was still unsure of what my mom might do or say to Rob or his mom.

I hadn't told Rob yet because I needed several days to soak in the gravity of the situation and figure out what in the heck I was going to do with my life. Hearing people's opinions didn't matter. I didn't believe in abortion, and I didn't like the thought of someone else raising my baby, so adoption was out of the question. I couldn't stand the thought of my kid wondering one day why his or her mom gave up her baby. The only thing I knew, from the minute I found out I was pregnant, was that I was going to be a mom – a young mom, but I didn't care. I loved this baby so much already! I knew there was **A Purpose** for why it had happened at this particular time in my life and I was going to embrace it and do the best I could.

I chose to take Dave with me to tell Rob the news. We arrived at Rob's house and I sat in the car while Dave went to get him to come out. He seemed surprised as he walked to my car. We hadn't really seen each other much since the breakup. We had both gotten good at avoiding each other at school. We knew each other's schedules and I took alternate routes in the hallways to intentionally avoid seeing him. We did have one class together, but we sat on opposite sides of the room and didn't have to communicate. In fact, for that class, I didn't even look in his direction.

I snapped out of my thoughts as he got to the car and I got out. We both sat down on the tailgate of his truck and after some small talk, I finally told him he was going to be a daddy. He looked a little shocked but not completely surprised because we both knew we hadn't always been careful. His only request was for me not to tell his mom. He wanted to do it. I agreed. It wasn't my place to tell her.

We didn't have a lot to talk about so we both sat there quietly. I said, "Well, I don't know what I'm going to do, but my mom knows, and she said she would help me however she could." I told him I still wanted to graduate from high school because my older brothers had both quit school and I wanted to be the first one in our family to graduate. He agreed and told me I should. I told him if he didn't want to be a part of the baby's life he didn't have to, and that I wouldn't ask him for any money. I told him I had family that was always willing to help and I could work as well. I told him I would figure it out. He told me he didn't know what he wanted and that he was supposed to be joining the Air Force. We didn't have much else to say, so I told him I needed to go. I'm sure I gave him a lot to think about. He and Dave talked for a few minutes and then we left. As we drove off, I watched him sitting there on the tailgate by himself, looking lonely and lost in thought, and wondered what he was thinking.

A few months went by and I didn't hear anything from him. I went about my business and did my own thing. I knew his mom knew because she had reached out to me, but she wasn't supportive. She thought we were too young to be parents and told me point blank that I would be ruining our lives and that I really needed to choose another option. However, I had already decided that I wouldn't let anyone influence my decision. I can be a very persistent and hard-headed person, and no one was going to tell me what to decide about something this big and that involved my future.

Even though mom had moved back to Sulphur Springs, I still wasn't living with her. Mom's husband didn't want me living with them. For all the years I had avoided living with them because I didn't like him, I guess now that he had the upper hand and was supporting my mom, he told her I couldn't live with them. I was pregnant and was going to be a mom. He told her I was 16, about to be 17, had made some adult decisions on my own, so I needed to figure it out on my own.

I had been fine staying at my uncle's, but I didn't want to overstay my welcome. I thank God for good friends. I had a school friend named DJ, and even though she was a year younger, we were close friends. She confided in me and I trusted her with a lot of my personal problems, too. I also met her sister, Crissy, and we soon became good friends as well. Their mom was a single mom and one day without me even pursuing it, they asked me to move in with them. They had shared with their mom what I was going through and she told them to tell me that if I needed a place to stay, they would be happy to let me live with them. At first I hesitated. Living with family is one thing, but I didn't know how well it would work – living with a friend and her family. However, I decided I would take them up on the offer, and it worked out great. It was as if I had sisters!

June and July went by and I turned 17 that July. I needed money and was working full time and as many overtime hours as I could that summer. Any free time I did get, I would hang out with friends. I was also going to church pretty often, and I was staying out of trouble. I still hung out with some of my friends at parties, but I was always the designated driver. I took care of everyone. I guess I was practicing on being maternal. Occasionally, my mom would go with me to my appointments but most of the time, my girlfriends went with me. We would also go on midnight runs or late-night cravings for Sonic and Taco Bell. It was good to have them with me all the time. It kept my mind off of being lonely. I did miss Rob, but every time a thought of him came to mind, I shut it down immediately. I reminded myself I was living for the little baby growing inside of me and I didn't have time to be sad or look back on the past.

One night in late August, Chrissy, DJ, and I decided to go to a revival at church so we all got dressed up. The service was great, and the sermon had been good, but then the preacher started making an alter call. DJ was a little emotional during this time because we had been watching people give their lives to God. It was pretty amazing! All of a sudden, the preacher started saying that there was someone there who needed to forgive someone. The preacher said, "The Lord wants you to know – if you can forgive this person tonight, He can quickly turn your situation around. He will make all things new; you just have to let it go and let God work on your behalf."

We all stood there listening to the preacher. I was getting a little hot and felt uncomfortable – as if he might be referring to me. Rob came to my mind, but I ignored the fact that the preacher might have been talking to me. I thought "God can't turn this around because too much has happened during the months since we broke up." I thought, "We will never be together again. Besides,

I just don't think I could forgive him and start over. I do love him, but it will never work out." Thought after thought kept running through my head and finally the preacher stopped and looked at me. As our eyes locked, he said, "Young lady, could you come here to the pulpit?" I looked all around and behind me hoping he was talking to someone else but unfortunately, he wasn't. I pointed at myself and asked him, "Me?" He smiled and said, "Yes please; I want to pray with you." I hate being the center of attention. I felt my face turning red and feeling hot. I said, "Okay," but before I could move, DJ grabbed my hand. She was bawling and said, "I'll go with you." Chrissy grabbed my other hand and we all three went up to the front.

The preacher said, "Sweetie, the Lord wants you to know that if you can forgive whoever hurt you, He will turn everything around and you will be amazed at what He can do. You just have to forgive and let the hurt go. God will heal the pain." I didn't know this man, he didn't know Rob had hurt me, but God knew what I had gone through. In that instant, I knew God was telling me through this preacher that I needed to forgive Rob. He had me repeat after him, "I forgive this person who has hurt me. I let it go and give it to God. No more anger and bitterness, no more hate. It goes – in Jesus' name." I won't go into all the details of the whole prayer, but after it was said and done, we were all weeping. We had makeup running down our cheeks, and we had seen each other's ugly cry faces. He even prayed over them since they were already up there. We all got to experience God in a big way that night. When the church service was over, all three of us left there excited and full of peace. We couldn't stop talking about it and couldn't contain the joy we had just experienced. I felt like a huge weight had been lifted off of me. They both said how glad they were to have gone to the revival!

We got in my Mustang and headed back to their house, but not before we did our usual run through the main drag. Everyone always rode around on the weekends and would park up at the K-mart parking lot to hang out. It had been awhile since I had seen Rob. Honestly, I didn't know if he was still in town or had already left for boot camp. As we pulled through, we saw some of our friends wave us over. We pulled up and started talking to them. I noticed Rob's truck parked over there, too. We told our friends that we needed to change out of our church dresses, get a bite to eat, and then we would come back and hang out with them. As we started to drive off, I saw Rob wave, so I waved back. Then DJ said, "Melissa, he's waving for you to go over there." I slowly drove my car over to the area of the lot where he was parked. When we pulled up, he came over to the driver's side of the car and said, "Hey, you look nice all dressed up! Where have you been?" I told him we had just left the church. By the look on his face, I'm sure he thought that was weird for a Saturday night. I told him we had been to a revival. He asked if I was sure I was pregnant because I still wasn't showing. I said, "I'm huge!" but honestly, unless I told you I was pregnant, you wouldn't have known it. He told me not to be starving his baby and reminded me that I was eating for two. I didn't have a lot to say and I was still shocked that he even wanted to talk to me in the first place. I told him that we were going home to change and eat since we hadn't eaten in a while. Before we could drive off, he asked me if he could call me and told me that he wanted to meet up at some point to talk about the baby. I told him I was staying with DJ and

Crissy and that he could call me at their house. He wrote down the phone number, smiled really big at me and waved good-bye. I couldn't help but be a little puzzled about the whole thing. In some strange way, he seemed different that night. He hadn't made any effort to reach out to me or find me or talk to me in three months and all of a sudden, he wanted to talk.

DJ said, "Melissa, what did that preacher say tonight? If Rob was the one you needed to forgive, and you did it, then God may be already turning things around." I said, "Wow, that was fast!" I had so much peace about what had happened in church that night that I had decided it was in God's hands and whatever happened next, I was letting God take full control. I was just going to step aside and not try to do things my way.

The next day, Rob called while I was at work, so I called him as soon as I got home. We talked for a few minutes to make plans to grab dinner together and talk. We decided to go to a place in Greenville, Texas, about 30 minutes away, since the food choices in Sulphur Springs weren't the best. I also didn't want the drama if people saw us out together. While we ate, he asked questions like how I was feeling, how the pregnancy was going, and if I knew whether I was having a boy or a girl. Then he told me he had decided not to join the Air Force because he wanted to be a part of the baby's life. He didn't want to be an absent father. He told me that he had gotten a better job than the one he had in high school and that the reason he hadn't been around was because he was working a lot of hours and lots of overtime. He, too, was saving money for the baby's needs. He really wanted to be there for his kid. I asked him what that meant, and the bomb shell was dropped. He told me he wanted joint custody.

Wait a minute!!!! NO, I don't think so!!!

I quickly lost my cool! This was my baby and had been this whole time! He wasn't about to come along now and tell me he wanted my baby six months of the year and I would only get them the other half of the year. Protective mother-bear in me came out quickly. "Look, I'm not trying to upset you." he said calmly. "You're pregnant, just relax. I just want you to know that I want to be a part of the baby's life. It doesn't have to be joint custody, but I'd like to work something out because I want to be involved. It's my kid, too, and I want to have a part in their life. We can figure out the details later. Let's not fight about it now." I was still unsure and had my guard up. I was not falling for any funny business, and he needed to know he wasn't getting my baby without a fight. After we left the restaurant, we did some baby shopping, but we didn't buy much because we still didn't know whether to shop for a boy or a girl.

He dropped me back off at my friend's house and asked if he could go with me to my next appointment – which was coming up that week. I told him no because I thought it would be weird that we weren't together as a couple and I didn't want him there, in case the doctor had to check me. However, I did tell him they were supposed to do a sonogram at the next visit to determine the sex of the baby, and I would let him borrow the sonogram video.

He agreed that would be okay. We didn't talk the next few days but on the day of the appointment, he called to remind me he wanted to see the video. We both decided it would be easier for me to drop it off at his house when I finished at the doctor's office. The baby didn't cooperate so the doctor still wasn't able to tell me the sex of the baby, but he did say the baby had healthy organs. I got to hear the baby's heartbeat and he said the baby was growing appropriately. All in all, the appointment went well. I dropped the sonogram video at Rob's house and we made a plan for him to return it to me.

After a few days, Rob called and suggested that I come over for dinner instead of him bringing the sonogram back to me. He said he would cook for me. A little hesitantly, I agreed. I didn't know that he knew how to cook!

Rob's mom was out of town when I went over to Rob's, but he had indeed cooked! He had made us tacos. He turned on the sonogram and asked me about it. I explained everything the doctor had pointed out on the video. He said he was happy and that it was starting to feel real. I told him, "Yeah, you should feel this baby kick! It's definitely real!" We had a nice visit and we talked and laughed together. It felt good to be around Rob again. It was around 10:30p.m. when I told him I needed to leave. I could see something different in his eyes. It was as if he didn't want me to leave, but we both said good-bye and I drove off.

Not much time went by before we started finding excuses to see each other a few days a week to talk, and before I knew it, he told me he wanted us to get back together. He wanted to us to be a family. I remembered the words the preacher had said at the revival: God would turn it around, and He had – in just a short amount of time! The baby finally cooperated and on the first visit that Rob attended with me, they did a sonogram and told us we were having a boy. October arrived, and we had gotten our own apartment. We were nesting and preparing for the arrival of our son.

We were both working, and I was going to school as well. It was a busy year because it was my senior year of high school. Looking back on it now, I don't even know how we made it back then! I made $4.25 an hour working as a cashier at Winn Dixie. If I remember correctly, Rob made about $7.00 an hour as a "puller" (he rode around the warehouse on a tug pulling grocery orders off the shelves to load up on the trucks for convenient store deliveries) at Grocery Supply. We were pretty strapped financially since we didn't have help from anyone. I was thankful that neither one of us had car payments and that my dad paid my auto insurance, but other than that, we lived on the bare minimum. My dad was upset with me and went a few months without speaking to me when he found out I was pregnant. It wasn't until his grandson was born that he resumed speaking to me again. My mom and Rob's mom didn't have the financial means to help us. Rob's dad wouldn't have been able to help us either. We were truly on our own.

Twice, Rob asked me to marry him and, even though I knew in my heart I wanted to, I kept telling him we would, but we needed to wait because the timing wasn't right. He wanted to get married before the baby arrived, but with all the hours he was putting in at work and the time I spent at school and work, we couldn't come up with a day that worked for both of us. Time flew by and we didn't get to get married before our son arrived.

Since I was going to school full time and getting closer to my due date, my hours at the grocery store had been cut back. Rob took on as much overtime as he could to make up for my lost wages. I did manage, however, to work some and continued going to school. One Friday, our assistant principal asked me to go ahead and sign up for homebound school because he was concerned I would go into labor at school.

This turned out to be a good decision because that Sunday, the day we had been waiting for was finally here. I had been in labor all night at home that Saturday, and as the new day began, delivery of our son became imminent.

We arrived at the hospital and 5 hours and 20 minutes later, we welcomed our baby boy. He was 8 pounds of perfect and the best gift God had ever given me.

He has a purpose!

A person may have many ideas concerning God's plan for his life, but only the designs of his purpose will succeed in the end. Proverbs 19:21

Chapter 7

A New Life Begins

We were completely in love with this little guy! After we brought him home, we would lay him in our bed and both of us would just stare at him for hours while he slept. We were still very much babies ourselves. I was 17 and Rob was 18, but we made ourselves a promise that we were going to make this relationship work, no matter how hard it might be. I wanted to be the best mom I could be. I wanted motherhood for me to be different than what I had ever seen or known. I was going to strive to be the best I could for my son. Rob had the same thoughts, too. He wanted his son to have things that he never had and opportunities he never imagined. He wanted to be involved in every part of his son's life. We decided we were going to do life differently than anything either of us had ever seen growing up. The areas that we had missed out on and that our parents had lacked in, we were going to make up for it with our son – and any future children God blessed us with.

December came and went quickly. It was time for me to go back to school after being homebound for six weeks. I was overwhelmed with schoolwork and a colicky baby. Rob worked nights so I had to try to find a good balance for doing homework, working, and being a mom. During the time I had been on homebound, getting schoolwork done was a little easier because I had a teacher come sit at my house and wait for me to take tests and sometimes wait for me to complete the assignments. Sometimes he even entertained or held our son so I could get some schoolwork done. Nights were harder though because it was just me and the baby, when he screamed and cried the most, which made it hard to get anything done. I did a lot of homework bouncing my son on my knees or shoulders just to finish assignments. I often read out loud to him, too, because sometimes the sound of my voice would soothe him. He was learning a lot of twelfth grade schoolwork as an infant.

Since Rob and I both came from broken homes, getting married was a scary thought for me. I wanted to get married, but I was afraid it wouldn't last. All I had ever really seen growing up was dysfunctional marriages or relationships. I didn't want that for us, and I was truly terrified. Now that we had a baby in the mix, it was even more terrifying!

The one marriage I had always looked up to was my grandparents' marriage. That marriage lasted 60 years! I spoke with my grandma about it. You always want to seek relationship advice from someone who has been in a lasting relationship. I won't say what all we talked about it because it was a personal conversation that I hold dear to my heart, but when I left there, I felt better about marriage. I was at peace about taking the leap into marriage. Rob finally asked me again and this time, without any hesitation or excuses, I said, "YES!" I admitted to him that I had been scared of getting married because of what I had seen and known growing up. We made plans to go to the courthouse and have the Justice of the Peace marry us. It was all we could afford because we never had any extra funds. We lived from paycheck to paycheck and did without food sometimes so we could provide for our little guy's necessities. It was rough, but we did it. Our parents never knew, but sometimes all we could afford to eat was peanut butter and crackers because we had to buy diapers or formula or wipes. Anything for our son always came before our needs. We also wanted to prove to our parents that we could make it on our own.

I remember like it was yesterday. When things were getting tough and we were about to run out of diapers and formula, I did what I had always been taught to do in times of need. I would start praying for a miracle. It always worked out. Sometimes after those prayers, someone would show up at our doorstep with diapers, wipes, or formula. Rob's aunt blessed us several times and some-times my dad would send me some money in the mail and tell me to buy his grandson something. God always provided for us through the blessing of our loved ones without us ever even having to ask them for help. Prayer never fails.

We finally got married in the spring, a few weeks before my high school graduation. We had a few friends that wanted to be there, and both of our moms and our five month-old baby were in attendance as we exchanged our vows.

Life was busy and hectic, to say the least. Even though my dad had offered to pay for college, I opted to work full time. It was hard enough trying to do homework assignments and study for tests with a baby during the last semester of my high school. Plus, we were still unsure about what we would do for daycare since Rob worked nights. Our childcare options were limited since we didn't have a lot of funds with which to work. My thoughts were – once my son got a little older, I'd go to college.

I had a chance to work through JTPA (Job Training Partnership Act) where I learned basic office skills and proper office phone etiquette, which was very helpful. I was even selected as the Outstanding Participant of the Year for 1994. I received recognition and an award! I had to go to Texarkana to accept it, but it was a pretty big deal. They were impressed with my work and that I could balance full-time school while being a mom, and that I had graduated High School all in the same year. The program was temporary, and I had only been able to participate in it the second semester of my senior year, but I believe it helped me land a great job at the Medical Clinic that August, just a few short months after I had graduated from school. I loved the people at the clinic with whom I worked. Some of my coworkers were friends from high school and I made another really close friend there.

After working at the clinic for a few years, we were doing a lot better financially so we decided to start trying to have another baby. We were more prepared this time – a lot more so than the first time around for sure! We got pregnant and within a few weeks of being pregnant, I knew I had miscarried. I hadn't been far enough along to require a D & C (a surgery where all the fetal tissue is removed from the uterus to help prevent infection or heavy bleeding).

Time passed, and we kept on trying. We knew we wanted at least one more baby. We got pregnant again and this time I was already close to ten weeks along when one terrible night, I woke up because I thought I had to go to the bathroom. I felt wet, but we had a waterbed at the time so my first thought was that the bed was leaking. My second thought was that maybe I had peed in the bed. When I got out of bed and went to the bathroom, I noticed I had blood all over my legs and my gown. I was starting to freak out a bit when I went back to the bedroom and turned the light on. I called out for Rob and told him to look at the bed. It looked like someone had been murdered in our bed. There was so much blood!!!

Since I worked for the clinic in town, I called one of the doctors I worked for and his wife answered and said he was at the hospital making rounds but that she would call him and have him call me back. Within a few minutes he called me back and told me that we needed to meet him at the clinic. Rob drove me and we found out I had miscarried again, but this time I would need to have surgery.

We were heartbroken. We decided having more children was not in God's plan for our lives. We had our son and we were blessed, so we were going to stop there. We didn't think we could emotionally handle going through this painful episode again. I got back on birth control pills and we continued living life as usual. A few months, later I started to feel sick and tired all the time. I was throwing up morning, noon, and night, but I still hadn't missed a period so I was a little confused about what was going on. I talked to one of my nurse friends and she advised me to take a pregnancy test. One of my best friends from the clinic walked with me over to my OB/Gyn doctor. I ran in, took a test, and found out I was indeed pregnant. I was excited and yet a little nervous because we hadn't been trying. The doctor informed me it was fine. However, I would need to get off the birth control pills and start taking prenatal vitamins.

I wondered what Rob would think since the last miscarriage hit us really hard emotionally. I didn't know if he would be excited at all. We were so sure we were finished with trying to get pregnant that we had gotten rid of all our baby supplies. But God had other plans for us.

I got home that evening after work and didn't waste any time telling him I was pregnant again. He was indeed happy, but we agreed not to tell anyone until after the first trimester.

It was a brutal pregnancy. I was sick for seven months and was losing a significant amount of weight. At around the seven-month mark, I started having symptoms of a miscarriage again. My doctor put me on bed rest for a week and I prayed several times a day that I would go full term and that my baby would be healthy. I had a lot of anxiety and fear about it, but I knew that throughout my life, God had never let me down – and I knew He wasn't about to start then. I went full term and even five days later than my due date! My healthy daughter was born at 8 pounds, 15 ½ ounces! **She has a purpose!**

She was another amazing gift from God! I had always wanted sisters and even before I found out that my first child was a boy, I had hoped for a girl. Now I had my little girl. God definitely knew what He was doing. They came in the order He had planned, and it was perfect for us.

Our family was complete. We decided we would stop there. The Lord had blessed us with a boy and a girl. We couldn't be happier! It's not that we didn't want any more kids, but I had a lot of problems with endometriosis and the chances of having more miscarriages was a possibility we didn't want to take.

Having two children was a lot different than having just one. Even though our son was a little over three years older, it was a very challenging time. We were trying to get our routine down and keep our son on his same schedule, but the baby made it a little harder. It took a while, but we finally got things down to an art. Schedules were going smoothly and we were doing well in our jobs. We had our son in private school, but we kept having issues finding someone to babysit our daughter. Everyone got tired of her pretty quickly. She wasn't a bad baby, but she had ear infections all the time and as soon as her antibiotic ran out, she had another ear infection. On top of that, she had stomach issues causing her to throw up a lot due to the fact that she was lactose intolerant. I was blessed to be able to quit my job and stay home with her when she was six months old. After she was a year old, she finally got tubes in her ears and was a much happier child – perhaps because she could actually hear us.

I love motherhood more than anything, and I never once thought of it as a burden. I sometimes doubted my parental abilities, and I would second guess some of the decisions I made, but I never once regretted having my babies. I learned how to cook really well, how to bargain shop, take care of our finances, and I got good at making crafts. The private school our son went to always had little parties and we couldn't afford to buy the party favors all the time for those parties, so all the cooking and craft shows I watched during this time at home with my daughter paid off. It was a great year off of work and it was nice to be able to stay at home – something I hadn't had the luxury of doing with our son because we needed both of our paychecks in order to survive.

After staying home for a year, I decided it was time for me to go back to work. We were both tired of renting and wanted to buy a house. We knew that in order to do that we needed more income and job stability so, without any hesitation, I decided to start looking for a job. I found a job that paid pretty decent wages and had good benefits, and I met some awesome new coworkers. I hadn't been working there very long when our daughter had an accident.

My daughter was a totally different child than our son. She was into everything! She knew how to get into every childproof cabinet, climbed on everything, and always ended up with bruises and black eyes. She was just her own little person! She was a very curious one, and she was a little spoiled. Even our son always let her have her way – not because we told him to, but because he always had a soft spot for her.

One Sunday in October, when she was 18 months old, we were at my Uncle Roy's house celebrating the family's October birthdays. I was in the kitchen with my mom and aunt getting everything together to eat soon. I was working on a big kitchen island making a salad and my aunt had a roast, either still cooking or keeping warm, in a crock pot on the countertop. My curious daughter, who was supposed to be sitting in the living room with all the other kids, had snuck out and came into the kitchen without our knowledge. As I was chopping the contents for the salad, I noticed the crock pot move. I looked over and there was my daughter, tugging on the cord to the crock pot. Since most kitchen island outlets plug on the side or underneath, it was low enough for her to reach.

I told her "No!" and put down my knife so I could go get her and take her back to the living room with the rest of the kids. The next events happened too fast to prevent, but I watched in what seemed to be slow motion. We couldn't get to her fast enough and she had that crock pot pulled over and on top of her in a split second. I can still hear her excruciating screams and the sound of her crying in my memories like it just happened, even though it's been over 21 years.

In that split second, I felt so helpless and incompetent. My mom and I grabbed her and started stripping her clothes off. You could see her skin boiling through her clothes. She was in severe pain and kept screaming, "Mommy!" I know she wanted me to help her, but I didn't know how. My sister-in-law called 911. I was in shock; I could hear words being said and my daughter's piercing screams, but I couldn't think straight. My mom was yelling at me to call my husband since he was working that Sunday, then she told me to snap out of it – my daughter needed me. My mom had taken my daughter, put her in a tub, and started pouring cool water on her while we waited for emergency services. My sister-in-law helped me contact my husband at work. He told me he would meet us at the emergency room.

After the ambulance arrived, the emergency crew started to open bottled water and pour it over her burns. They took us to the emergency room and after the doctor looked at her, he ordered some morphine for pain. He said she was going to have to be flown by care flight to the burn unit at Parkland Hospital in Dallas. This was one of the hardest days of my life. I watched my 18-month-old cry and reach for her daddy as they loaded her onto a stretcher and strap her in for her helicopter ride. She was crying and all she wanted was her daddy. I have seen my husband tear up a time or two before, but this day was very emotional for us. She was hurting, and we were both crying because she didn't understand that what they were doing was actually helping her. I imagined what my mom must have felt like the day they sent me by care flight to Dallas. My husband said it was miserable – having to experience watching a girl he loved being taken by helicopter in serious condition, not once, but twice. This time, I'm sure it hurt even worse because this was his baby girl. There is nothing like watching your baby suffer and not being able to do anything about it. As a parent, you would jump in front of a bullet, fight off a pack of wild animals, and give your last breath for your kids. Right then, and at that moment, we were hurting, yet helpless. There wasn't anything we could do. We were going to have to drive from Sulphur Springs to Dallas – an hour and a half drive – to the hospital, but we had to run home to get clothes because we were told they would keep her in the hospital a couple of days. We were very fortunate that my aunt just "happened" to be in the Dallas area that day. She was a chaplain and had gone over to see someone and pray with them. During all the chaos, my brother had called her to ask if she could go to Parkland and be there when our baby girl arrived. We were worried that she would be traumatized by being around strangers while in excruciating pain and we didn't want her to feel alone. My brother knew I would want my daughter to see a familiar face and be comforted by someone she knew until we could get there. I am so blessed I have a big family who is always ready and willing to be there for each other.

When we arrived, the doctors told us our daughter had first, second, and third degree burns on her right arm, shoulder and the right side of her abdomen and thigh. They said she was very fortunate it didn't get on her face or the parts of her body where she had major internal organs. They also said it was good that we had taken the clothes off of her; otherwise, they would have burned into her skin. The cool water my mom had poured over her had been good thinking as it kept her skin from boiling. I can't even begin to describe how crazy it was, but I know very well that, even though it was a freak accident, God was watching over her. Every doctor we encountered and talked to said this could have been so much worse!

Some people made comments to us like: if God is such a good God, why he would let something like this happen to a little girl? My answer is simple, even though it's hard to make people fully understand. God is a good God and He doesn't cause bad things to happen. Yes, He is all powerful, but the Bible says in:

³³ And everything I've taught you is so that the peace which is in me will be in you and will give you great confidence as you rest in me. For in this unbelieving world you will experience trouble and sorrows, but you must be courageous, [for I have conquered the world!"]

What I understand, or my take on this is that we must all go through things and, as awful as it is sounds, kids will have to go through things, too. One of my questions when I get to heaven will be: Why do kids have to go through pain? But throughout the whole ordeal, I wasn't angry or mad at God. I was grateful, even though my daughter was hurting and in pain, that it hadn't been worse or fatal. I was happy that she was alive and that none of her internal organs had been harmed.

There is not one person on this earth that can say they have not been through a trial or experienced something bad. I understand some people don't know to seek God and gain something from it. Maybe their situation wasn't as bad, or perhaps they didn't consider it as a trial in life, but we've all gone through tough times. God didn't cause her accident and He doesn't cause pain or accidents. However, He does carry us through all our bad times. During the times we need Him the most, He is with us and He never leaves us. He provides us comfort, regardless of what the world throws at us.

Long story short, my daughter healed nicely – and sooner than the doctors expected. That was in the fall of 1998 and now, at 22 years old, she only has a few scars that are visible. She healed so well that the part still visible today is only on her arm. The other parts show no visible evidence that she was ever burned. I give God the praise that she didn't have to endure burns that needed surgery, that she healed so quickly, and that she didn't have burns close to internal organs that would have caused other, more serious health problems. She is one tough young lady, and when people who see it and ask her about it, she gladly tells them what happened.

Thank God she doesn't remember all the pain she went through, but the experience has made her into the person she is today. For a few weeks we had to take her to Parkland Hospital in Dallas for whirlpools and scrubbing treatments twice a week. The doctors said it would be painful, but they taught us how to bathe her using a scrubber to keep the burns clean. We literally had to scrape off the old skin that could cause infection. This was hard on us because she screamed so severely when we had to do this. They also sent us home with some burn cream and, after every bath and treatment, we had to wrap her up like a little mummy so her skin wouldn't get infected, causing other problems. She squealed and cried so loudly that we would take our son to his room turn the music on and let him play Super-Nintendo with the volume really loud. We didn't want him hearing her suffering. My husband and I dreaded having to do this, and it took both of us to do it. No parent wants to see their child agonize in pain, and it was very painful for us emotionally because we were the ones having to physically hurt her in order to clean off the burns. With every treatment, we had to listen to her scream, "No, Mommy! No, Daddy! Please stop!" Even all these years later, when Rob and I remember those days, we tear up. It was one of the hardest things we had to endure as parents.

We told her when she turned 18 she could have cosmetic surgery if she wanted to so that people wouldn't ask her about her scars anymore or so that she wouldn't have any insecurities about them. Her response was, "NO! These have been with me most of my life and I am who I am because of these scars! I feel like a warrior with battle scars."

She has a purpose!

Chapter 8

My Heart has been Healed

In life, we must all choose how to react in tough times and when we go through trials.

As you can tell from my life, it hasn't been a walk in the park by any means. It hasn't all been easy, and I haven't always made the right choices. Some situations, I actually got myself into and the outcomes have not always been the easiest to handle. But in all those things, even though turning to God may not have been my first choice or the first thing I thought to do, I always sought Him eventually. Now as the years have progressed and I have gotten wiser, that's the first thing I think of doing.

When worry, fear, or anxiety come against me in times of trials, I call a friend or family member who believes in God and I tell them that I have a situation. I ask them to pray with me, or over me, or for them to stand in agreement with me that God will resolve whatever I'm going through. God hears our prayers regardless, but there is something powerful about prayer when you have others standing in faith with you. *Matthew 18:20 says For where two or three are gathered together in My name, I am there in the midst of them.*

After our daughter's freak accident, life in general continued. We bought our first house, took on some better paying jobs with better benefits, continued raising our kids, sold our first house, bought another one, and chased our kids around from ball field to ball field. We tried to support them in all of their extracurricular activities. In the craziness and busiest times of our lives, where we almost never had any spare time, we decided we would build a house. That probably wasn't the wisest decision we had ever made.

In 2006, we bought land, and construction began on our dream home. I call it our first dream home because you should never stop dreaming. In 2007, we sold the current house and our new house was completed about six months later. We loved our custom-built home, the neighborhood, and our neighbors. However, with all the traveling we did for year-round sports to support our kids, maintaining the house, yard, and land was tough because we were rarely home.

In addition, my husband's job was starting to cause chaos with our home life schedule. He had worked nights for years and had finally worked his way up to working the day shift. This change was supposed to be permanent, but after just a short time, the company's upper management started making some changes and it looked like he would be going back to the nightshift. This new schedule didn't make us happy. We wanted to enjoy every bit of time we had left with the kids. Our son was now a junior in high school and we wanted to soak up every minute we had left with him at home. With my husband's work schedule changing, it would mean less time for him to watch our kids play ball, cheer, and all the other activities in which they were involved. He promised me he wasn't going to work nights permanently and started looking for other jobs. Nevertheless, in the interim, we started to feel the strain a bit. Because he couldn't make every game, that sometimes that left me to have to choose which kid I would go watch while the other one was playing without a parent there. Almost simultaneously, I started having some health issues and wasn't feeling very well.

My regular doctor recommended I see a cardiologist. I was starting to feel winded and have some chest pains, but I thought it was just anxiety from all the stress in our lives. The cardiologist had me wear a heart monitor for a week and told me he was going to schedule me for more tests. I thought, "I'm only 34. How can I have anything wrong with my heart?" At the same time, I knew that I hadn't felt "right" in a couple of months. If I was climbing stairs, I would get light-headed and feel like I was going to pass out.

One night, a very strange thing happened when I was asleep. I thank God that Rob was off work that night because I know he remembers me doing this. It had never happened before and hasn't happened since. I had gone to bed with chest pains but thought that if I got a good night's rest, I would get up feeling better the next day. What woke me up from a deep sleep was that I wasn't able to breathe. It felt as if someone was smothering my face and chest. I couldn't catch a breath and then I started to panic, which made my situation worse. I jumped up and started running around the room. Because my husband was a supervisor over several employees, he had undergone emergency training to treat people in various emergency situations. He jumped up out of bed, grabbed me, and started talking me out of my panic. He said, "Put your arms above your head and try to breathe now." Within seconds, I could catch a breath and snapped out of it. To this day, I can't say what happened, but I literally thought I was dying. I had always heard a heart attack felt like a heaviness and what woke me was a heaviness in my chest. I feel like that led to the panic attack – if that's what it was.

A day or two went by and the chest pains still continued. I was so tired of those chest pains! I was still wearing the heart monitor (which wasn't comfortable by the way), and I wouldn't know my results until after the doctor had time to review the tests, so I still had several days of waiting. The doctor's concern stemmed from the fact that heart disease was very common on my dad's side of the family. Several of my uncles, aunts, and a few of my cousins have had heart surgeries. Therefore, the doctor was afraid to rule anything out – no matter what my age was.

One night, I went to bed praying and asking God to heal me. I prayed for a good night's sleep and for the chest pains to stop. I also asked God to heal my heart if anything was wrong with it. We can do that! We can ask God for total and complete healing – we just have to believe it when we ask for it. From the time I was a little girl, my mom's side of the family has always taught me that God is our healer and all we have to do is ask.

.

Romans 8:11 New International Version (NIV)

*¹¹ And if the Spirit of him who raised Jesus from
the dead is living in you, he who raised Christ from
the dead will also give life to your mortal bodies
because of his Spirit who lives in you.*

I love how the Word of God says we can speak life into someone, or even for ourselves, because that same spirit that raised up Christ from the dead lives in us, and He has given us that authority!

On this particular evening, I had finally drifted off to sleep when suddenly I didn't feel like I was asleep anymore. I saw my grandpa standing there in my bedroom. He was singing and asking me to come to him. At that moment, I remembered what he sounded like, how he used to sing in his church when I was younger, and how he used to wave me up to the front of the church to sing – just as he was waving at me in this dream.

As he was telling me to come towards him, I started thinking, "He's been gone so long! Oh, how I've missed him." I wanted to get to him and hug him, but there seemed to be a force of some kind that wouldn't let me get close enough to touch him. He kept telling me to keep singing. It was a Spanish hymn and though I won't translate the whole song, in English, the name of that Spanish hymn would be *"Come to Him."* The song, in short, has a verse that says: If, in your body, you feel like you're dying that He (GOD) will be your

Heavenly doctor and Savior. All you have to do is come to Him and He will heal you. The song really makes more sense and sounds better in Spanish, but the verse repeats over and over "Come to Him."

Without knowing the whole song, it may sound a little weird, but this song was telling me that I didn't have to be concerned about my health or be afraid. All I had to do was come to God, like I had that night in prayer, and that God was my healer. I started singing the song over and over with my Grandpa. I was crying, too. I hadn't heard that song in over 20 years. It was one they used to sing at his church, but for some reason, that night I remembered it in my dream. My grandpa smiled one last smile and said, "There is nothing wrong with your heart. You've been healed." I woke up singing and looked for him in the room where he had been standing. He was gone, but my pillow was wet where I had been crying.

I have an uncle who interprets dreams so after I woke up that morning, I called my mom. I asked her if she would call him and find out what that dream meant. When I spoke with her again, she said he told her it was an angel that had appeared to me. He looked like my grandpa so I wouldn't be afraid, but the angel was giving me a message from God that He had healed me. Repeating the song over and over was to be a reminder that no matter what we go through – whether sickness (or whatever we are faced with) – all we have to do is go to Him (GOD) with it and He will take care of it. I know that some skeptics might think I'm looney, but I will tell you this: After that night, I didn't have any more chest pains like I had been having earlier. Then when I went back to see the doctor and had more tests run, they couldn't find anything wrong with my heart!

And something else: Several years previous to this situation, I had been told by two separate doctors that I had mitral valve prolapse, a condition where the blood doesn't travel well from one chamber of the heart to the next and it used to cause a little regurgitation in my heart. However, after the night I had the dream and then all the tests were run, even that was gone! That means that not only was my present heart condition healed, but an ailment that I had already had for several years was also healed! God is so good!!! My heart had been completely healed!

I serve a good God, a God who heals. People can say I'm crazy or think whatever they want, but you will never convince me otherwise. I know I keep repeating myself but **I have a purpose!**

Time and time again, God has never let me down. I've been blessed in so many ways. After all this was behind us, we resumed our life of craziness. We started making college visits for our son and my husband had gotten a few job offers. The only negative in all this was he was going to have to take a pay cut and drive out of town to work. At the time, that was fine since his current job was cutting into our family time, and family time was more important to us than money.

We started talking about selling the house. We knew that after our son left for college it would only be three years before our daughter would be leaving for college, too. My husband took the job out of town and we sold the house shortly after our son left for college in the fall of 2012. We sold the house faster than expected, so we opted to rent until we could decide what would be next in our future.

The job my husband took had a great opportunity for advancement. In fact, even though Rob originally took a cut in pay at the beginning, it was only a short time until he had gotten a promotion and a raise so that he was making even more money than at his previous company. The bad thing about this new job was that the atmosphere seemed to be affecting his health. He would come home and shower, but when he cleaned his ears or blew his nose, black "stuff" was coming out. Even then, when he went to bed, he would leave a dark colored outline on our sheets from where he had laid. It was as if he was sweating out the impurities that must have been prominent in his work environment. It was really concerning. Then he began having some small health issues. I hated to suggest he leave his job, but I didn't like the quality of air he was breathing in at work. Even a doctor suggested that he needed to find something else because what we were describing didn't sound safe to be around. He stuck with it for a few years and, in the meantime, we focused on our daughter and all her sports and activities. We didn't want to miss out on any of her events, and we knew from what we experienced with our son, it would only be a matter of time before she would be leaving the nest, too.

Life kept us busy: his job, our daughter's activities, and making time to visit our son in College Station. With all these changes, we started noticing that getting older wasn't much fun. We started having a few small health issues, although thankfully, there was nothing too major. My husband had broken a wrist that required two surgeries, I had to have a hysterectomy, he had to have an emergency appendectomy, I had to have my gall bladder removed and he had to have a surgery on his shoulder. It seemed like if it wasn't me, it was him. It was getting annoying – and quite expensive.

Chapter 9

Where Do We Go from Here?

Our daughter's senior year arrived. Time was flying by so quickly! We had already toured a few schools and she had decided she wanted to attend Texas Tech in Lubbock. That February, four months before graduation, we paid a deposit for her dorm. We wanted the choice of schools to be her decision, but without our daughter's knowledge, Rob and I had secretly been praying that she would reconsider and either go to College Station to be close to her brother or choose Texas A&M Commerce to be closer to us. It was scary leaving your firstborn four hours from home, but the thought of letting the baby go off even farther was more terrifying. With the last six weeks of her senior year looming, we felt like our prayers had been answered when she told us she wanted to go to Commerce instead of Lubbock. Even though we lost a big percentage of the deposit we put down for her dorm, we weren't disappointed. It was going to be worth it – and quite a relief – to know she would only be 20 miles down the road, in case she had an emergency.

She graduated from high school the spring of 2015. The summer came and went quickly, and before we knew it, we were moving her into her dorm in Commerce. Even though she wasn't far, this momma still couldn't hold back the tears, knowing her baby had grown up and was out on her own.

In 23 years, Rob and I had never really had a chance to be on our own. Remember we went from dating, to living together, and into parenthood without a honeymoon phase – or even a getting-to-know-you phase.

After moving her in and decorating her dorm room, we came home to an empty house. We were so tired, supper didn't even sound good. We both sat down on the couch and looked at each other. I was an emotional wreck – both of my babies were gone! I know it's just a part of life. You do the best you can to raise them and prepare them for the real world. We couldn't have asked for better kids, but, like many mommas, I was having an issue with letting them go.

Because we were so young when we started having kids ourselves, we were super strict with our kids. My son used to get upset at how overprotective we were. We made sure to check out the kids they were hanging out with, and they didn't have as much freedom as some of their friends had. We weren't as naïve as our parents had been. He would make comments to us that we were the youngest parents of all of his friends – but the strictest. My husband always told him, "We aren't stupid! We know what we were doing at your age and we won't allow it. We want life to be better for you kids."

But here in this moment, my husband and I quit reminiscing and said, "Where do we go from here?" We knew we had a purpose, but we also knew it was for more than just being our kids' parents. Life was for more than what we had done the last 23 years raising kids, but we couldn't quite figure out what that was.

We had been attending church in Royse City and had made several friends and decided that we needed to get more involved. In the past, we had too much going on with the kids – year-round sports, travel sports, games, and tournaments – to fully commit to a church. I'm not saying it was right because we tried to teach our kids that God came first and to put Him before everything. However, as I reflect now, I don't think we were demonstrating that as well as we should have. We did make sure that if they didn't have ball games or tournaments that they couldn't miss church. It's one of those things that when you're in the middle and doing the best you can, you think you're doing it right. Then after it's said and done, you think, "I should have done that differently." I can't say my kids ever went through a rebellious stage and refused to go to church. Even when my son was in College Station and on his own, he found a church and attended regularly. My daughter is still in college and married, but she and her husband attend church regularly. I guess we didn't completely fail as parents!

Rob and I were trying to get used to our new-found freedom so we decided to serve and give our time by joining the "Dream Team" at our church. This is a group of volunteers that help out in areas needed. Our church was a fairly new church and, at the time, it was a "mobile" church. We were temporarily renting an existing facility that was used for other purposes the other days of the week so we had to "set up and break down" the location every Sunday. We decided to join community groups and leadership groups through our church, since now we could focus on ourselves and make friends outside of our usual baseball/softball moms and dads.

Not only were we making new friends, we were also digging deeper into God's Word and trying to figure out who we were – other than just being someone's mom or dad. We started to enjoy our empty nest and began reconnecting with each other. Instead of the normal hustle and rush to be somewhere, we were now able to start making time for ourselves, including date nights, overnight stays here and there, and just enjoying less parental responsibility.

As we took the leadership classes at church, they asked us to make a full year commitment to dig deeper into God's Word. Through the classes, we read books that could help improve leadership skills and help us grow in our relationship with God. We met once a month, had homework assignments to help improve ourselves, and help us discover who we were – individually, as a couple, and corporately – in Christ. We learned about some of our strengths and weaknesses and discussed areas where we could use some improvement. We made dream boards and started to actually dream about our futures. We got to hear some excellent guest speakers and learned so much – about God, about our church, and most importantly, about ourselves. It is good to invest in yourself in order to learn how to become the best you that you can be.

One of the books I read in one of the leadership groups really made an impression on me. When it came to making effective changes in my life, I always had good intentions but held back a lot because I lacked courage and boldness. This time, I decided I didn't have anything to lose and I was ready to make the necessary changes that could better my life.

As you may know, <u>when you decide to live completely for God, there will be opposition from the enemy</u>. Regardless of how large or how little, he doesn't want to relinquish whatever hold he may have had on you. He will fight you with whatever he can throw at you!

Even though some of these things will be tough to admit, just saying that I wanted to be "fully in" with my walk with God wasn't enough. I was going to have to let go of some ugliness I had let build up in my heart.

I wanted to relinquish insecurity. I had always been insecure – from the time I was old enough to be aware of my surroundings. I always thought I wasn't good enough because of my skin color, my lack of not having whatever everyone else had and, even as I became an adult, I felt insecure about the lack of education I had. The enemy is always trying to whisper into your thoughts that you're not good enough. You'll find out later in my story where a lot of this insecurity came from. However, it is possible to shake off the lies he throws at you by using the Bible as your weapon against those thoughts.

Romans 12:2 (AMP)

And do no not be conformed to this world but be transformed and progressively changed by the renewing of your mind, so that you may prove what

the will of God is, that which is good and acceptable
and perfect.

I also had to let go of hate. I had grown up with so much hate inside me – towards family members who had hurt me both physically and emotionally. Looking back at it now, it seems I hated people, situations and circumstances in my life. I'm not proud to admit this, but a part of me even hated my mom. Later, I will explain why, but I knew I had to let it go. When you are trying to give up an emotion like hate, the enemy will flood you with strong memories of things and people in your past and sometimes even make you relive why you hated those people. You have to remember and stand firm on what the Bible says. Then say (and keep repeating) to yourself, "I will not hate." I kept saying, "I choose to love my mom. I will love those who have hurt me. I will choose love, not hate."

Proverbs 10:12

Hatred stirs up conflict, but love covers all wrongs.

For me, one of the hardest things to let go of was unforgiveness. This, too, was directed toward family members and loved ones who had hurt me. Forgiving is hard because we can say all day long "I forgive," but our memory doesn't forget. During the times when you want to forgive, it seems like your memory goes into overdrive replaying all the wrongs that have been done to you. You want to forgive, but it's hard to forget. In times like these, it is best to remember: Forgiveness is not about accepting or excusing someone's behavior. You are not saying it was okay that they hurt you, or that you're okay with what they did or even may still be doing. You are simply saying "I'm forgiving you for myself, because I'm through letting you have that much control over my life! I forgive you for me – not to let you off the hook and not to let you hurt me again. I'm forgiving you so that I can have peace and move on with my life!" Forgiveness is about letting go to prevent their behavior from destroying you.

If you want to be happy, you can't have unresolved feelings of unforgiveness. Just do your part and forgive. The rest is on that person and God. He is your vindicator and if we do what He wants us to do, that's all we should be concerned about on our part. That doesn't mean you have to fall into the trap and let that person hurt you over and over. You can forgive, then keep a healthy distance. You do not have to continue to be involved with a person who has the habit of hurting people. If necessary, you may have to close the door to repeat offenders. I know I have.

Matthew 6:14-15 (NIV)

For if you forgive men when they sin against you,
your heavenly Father will also forgive you. But if
you do not forgive men of their sins, your Father
will not forgive your sins.

The next piece of baggage that had to go was jealousy. I dealt with this a lot! In my life, I have found it hard to trust people because I have been hurt in a lot of ways – from the time I was a kid till even now. This isn't the kind of jealousy that is like wishing I had what someone else had. This is jealousy caused by insecurity. This is the kind that comes from thinking I was not ever good enough. Growing up, I saw many relationships and how they ended, and I watched people cheat on each other. This can make you think everyone does it, which is another lie thrown at us by our enemy. Because I wanted to be a better person in this area, this scripture is one on which I have learned to rely.

2 Corinthians 5:17

Therefore, if anyone is in Christ, the new creation has come: The old has gone the new is here!

I also battled with some anger towards a family member who had wronged me emotionally in more ways than I would ever want to admit. It, too, needed to go.

James 1:20

For the anger of man does not achieve the righteousness of God.

Proverbs 29:11

A fool always loses his temper, but a wise man holds it back.

Oddly enough, within a few weeks of my decision to let go of all the ugliness I had been harboring for years, I started getting sick. It could have been a coincidence, but I doubt it. I was trying to be a better person and let go of the emotional grip the devil had on my life for so many years. I really believe the enemy had such a stranglehold on that part of me that he didn't want to let go without a fight.

It started in May of 2017. In the beginning and for a few weeks, it was minor things. Then a few days before my birthday in July, I started to get really sick – like seven weeks of "pure hell" sickness. I couldn't keep any food in my system. Regardless of what I ate or drank, everything would run right through me. I had a terrible pain in my right side. One doctor was convinced it was my appendix, but my tests for that came back normal. It was a miserable feeling. I was missing a lot of work, and I started disconnecting from friends and family. I didn't want to leave the house. My husband and I had already paid for a Disney vacation for just the two of us that July and we were both so excited about going. I had seen a doctor a few days prior to our trip and he had given me some medicine. He said it was just a virus that had to run its course, that I should be fine, and to go ahead and go on my trip.

The day we left, I felt great! The next day I started getting a little nauseous. Except for one day, the entire week in Florida was a total bust. I was so sick, I ended up in the emergency room. I'm not exaggerating when I say I thought I was dying. It was absolutely awful! I was so weak and lethargic. They gave me an IV and told me I was dehydrated and that it might be better just to get back home to Texas. I laid in the bed of our condo praying and crying because I felt so bad. I wanted to go home, but I felt too sick to think about the long ride home. My husband even mentioned sending me back home on an airplane and he would drive back, but I didn't want to be alone.

When we returned, I went to see my regular doctor. He ran tests and blood work. They said I had a severe gastrointestinal virus and it would have to run its course, which could take weeks or even months. The doctor warned me that those viruses could sometimes be fatal. He said if I got worse, he was going to put me in the hospital. They kept asking if I had been out of the country or anything of the sort because my symptoms seemed similar to those of people who had traveled beyond the borders of the United States and had gotten sick from contaminated food or water. I told them I had never traveled outside of the U.S.

It took everything out of me just to make the 45-minute trip to the doctor, and I was going once and sometimes twice a week, but I was getting worse instead of better. I was so weak and miserable. Even people at work were telling me I didn't look good or healthy. My skin color was changing, my eyes looked terrible and the weight was falling off of me for lack of being able to eat. I remember looking at my dream board where I wrote that I wanted to lose 35 pounds this year. I guess I should have been more specific about how I wanted to lose weight! With this sickness came other maladies: Vitamin D deficiency, low iron levels, and three rounds of strep throat. My immune system was so out of whack that I couldn't fight off any sickness. Even after I finally got over the strep, my throat continued to hurt. Then my neck and shoulders began to hurt, too. I was convinced it was from the stress of being sick for so long. I went to a back and neck doctor to get checked out and they found a slightly bulging disc. After six weeks of physical therapy, the back and neck pain got better, but I was still having problems with my throat hurting.

My doctor finally decided to send me to a specialist where, after having an endoscopy, he concluded it was esophagitis. I was given a prescription for this, too, but was still unable to eat. Months of being sick had gone by and I was down a total of 62 pounds. While I had needed to lose some weight, this wasn't a healthy way to do it! I sure did miss food, but the sight of food scared me because of the side effects. I was only able to drink my food. My husband was really worried because my body was looking super frail in a matter of just a few months and he knew I couldn't live forever on Jell-O, pudding, and water. He started buying me muscle milk shakes so that I could get some protein. Only a few close friends at the time knew of the severity of the issues, but I was told that the virus could have killed me. There were nights I laid in bed praying and asking God, "If this is my time Lord, please be with my family and give them peace. Comfort them, if they lose me." The enemy would torment my mind at bedtime. I was afraid and had a lot of anxiety. Several months of being sick can really take a toll on you mentally.

BUT, I'm alive and healthy because of a loving God who heals! There were days that, as a grown 41-year old woman, I would call my mom crying. I hurt, I was tired of not being able to keep food in my system, and I felt so weak. I would pray, cry, and read scriptures and healing books. I listened to worship songs over and over. The song, "Healer" by Kari Jobe was played hundreds of times during those months. I read the book, Healed from Cancer, by Dodie Osteen because it had a lot of healing scriptures in it and told about how she battled her sickness by standing on God's Word. I highlighted those scriptures and on days I felt really bad, I wrote them down and read them over and over. Even at work when I started feeling bad, I pulled out the paper I had written them on and kept reading them. Sometimes I felt so alone. No one outside of my home really knew how sick I was or how bad I felt. No one, except my husband, understood what I was going through. He would hold me as I cried myself to sleep at night. He would tell me he was sorry and that he felt bad for me. My husband is a fixer when it comes to his loved ones and it was hurting him to not be able to fix my situation. On the days I stayed home from work because I was too sick to be away from a bathroom, my husband would call me several times a day to check on me. Several days a week, he would not go to the gym after work because he didn't want to leave me alone any longer than he had to. He never really told me what his thoughts were during those months of me being sick, but I could see the concern on his face and I could hear it in his voice. We were supposed to be enjoying our empty nest and each other, but I was so sick that I couldn't even enjoy life! He was working, taking all the home responsibilities, and taking care of me – not letting me do anything. He would tell me, "I just want you to get better. This is only temporary; your healing is coming." I wanted to believe him, and I knew that he was right, but when you're going through the fire it's hard to bear the heat. It's easy for someone to encourage you when they're on the outside looking in, but when it's you, it's hard to stand firm and believe.

There were so many days I would pray and ask God, "Why me? Why do I have to suffer?" Some days, I would start to doubt and wonder if God was even listening to me. It seemed like every time I would start to let fear in or start letting myself think I wouldn't get better, I would hear a sermon that would tell me otherwise. Sometimes, a friend from church would shoot me an email or text me a word of encouragement, or my mom would call and give me scripture to remind me that God knew what I was going through and not to doubt that I would get my healing. God was using people around me to reach out when I was discouraged, and it always came when I felt the lowest. Since I hadn't told anyone of my illness, I knew it was God speaking to me through them.

I was sick from around May of 2017 until about February of 2018 before I finally started to see my symptoms begin to subside and I started feeling more and more like myself. On one particularly rough day during that time, I remember thinking that I felt so tired and sick, and sick of being sick and tired. However, I began to wonder: If I were to leave this earth, will I have made a difference? Will anyone notice that I was ever here? Did I exhibit the love I was put here on earth to demonstrate or will they not even miss me because I didn't impact their lives?

It was on that day that I was told something that I had never known! They told me that I always had something nice to say about people and that I may never know the impact I had made on their life. At the lowest time in their life, when they were ready to end it, I made them feel loved and worth something. I had made a difference in their life and they would be forever grateful. WOW! I didn't know that I had made an impact like that!

I realized that my purpose was just to be what God wanted me to be. I could take something as small and effortless as a compliment and make a difference in someone's life. I could encourage someone by telling them they matter and, no matter what their past was like, that God would forgive them and they didn't have to live in shame. I could hug a person that looked like they needed a hug. I could text someone a scripture or a word of encouragement when God put that person in my thoughts. I could send a "thinking of you" card or tell someone that was feeling unloved that they are loved. I could invite someone to church and take them out to lunch afterwards. Small random acts of kindness can and do go a long way.

Other than being an attack from the enemy, I honestly don't know the purpose behind being sick for all those months. I know we will all go through trials on earth. I don't know if I was supposed to learn something out of it, but I did learn to be grateful and appreciate the small things in life. Furthermore, I do know this: I drew closer to God in those nine months than ever before in my entire life. When I was a kid, teenager, and young adult, I hadn't realized how much of a difference I could make. Always before, I never felt like I mattered, but this time was different. I decided my purpose was not to be shy about who I am. I choose to be confident, to share the Word of God, and to tell everyone that we all have a purpose. I decided I'm going to enjoy every minute of every day of my life. I'm going to show and tell my loved ones how much I love them.

I remember seeing the faces of my family as they saw my health declining during those months when we would go eat after church. Sunday was usually our family day. After the kids grew up and had their own lives, getting to see them once a week is a highlight. On one particular Sunday, my son looked at my plate and said, "Momma, is that all you want to eat?" I said, "Yes, son. That's all I can eat." He looked at me with so much sadness in his eyes and asked me to be honest with him. He said, "Please don't keep anything from us. If this is more serious than you're letting on, we want to know." I was being honest. I was telling them everything the doctor had told me.

I had been pretty overweight for the last ten years and, after all the weight loss, my daughter hugged me on one occasion and said, "Momma, I feel your bones. You need to get to eating again. You don't feel healthy." I told her I wasn't starving myself on purpose; I just couldn't eat without it making me sick.

I share that because I watched how my sickness affected the people around me whom I love. It gave me a reason not to give up. I decided to dig my heels in and tell the enemy to get lost and take his weapons of sickness with him. My kids still needed me around, I still had a long life to live ahead of me, and I wasn't going to be sick forever. My husband and I still had a lot of things we wanted to do and accomplish together — and he needed me because we made a vow to grow old together. I had gone over and over in my mind for about a week or so after my kids had made comments about my health it was then that I decided that I was not only going to try to impact my family, but I was going to step outside my comfort zone and try to make an impact on other people's lives as well.

During that time of illness, one of my favorite scriptures that I said every day was:

Psalms 118:17

*I will not die but live and proclaim what the Lord
has done.*

Some people will spend their whole lives searching and wondering if they made a difference, but they won't take any action to try to find their purpose. Start with your family. Start in your home. Start by sowing seeds of encouragement and love to those closest to you, and then branch out.

Some people have a love or a heart for the elderly. Go to a nursing home and ask to read to those who want to be read to or play checkers with ones who like to play games. Love on the elderly.

If you have a heart for kids, find a boys and girls club and volunteer as a big brother or sister. Volunteer in the children's department at church. Kids today are always needing someone to mentor them and teach them that society's idea of love is not God's way. Love on some kids.

If you have a neighbor who is a single mom, offer to babysit so she can have some alone, or quiet time. Love your neighbor's kids and your neighbor. Perhaps for that young couple with kids who never get to go out because they might not be able to afford a sitter, offer to watch the kids for free for a few hours so the couple can reconnect and have a date night.

We all have a purpose. We all have a passion for something. Step out of your comfort zone and find your purpose.

In writing this book, I feel like my purpose is to share how good God is and has been to me. He has proven time and time again how much He loves me.

Even when I didn't feel like I was anyone, He was already working in me. He was already working on my heart to discover my purpose. If He did it for me, He can do it for you. He loves all his children the same. I'm not any better than anyone else. We are equally loved and created by the same Creator.

Am I perfect? Absolutely not!

Do I mess up? Every day! I'm thankful for God's grace.

Do I have a perfect life, marriage, family? No, no and no!

Have I failed people? Of course, that goes back to me saying I'm not perfect.

Am I always happy? Nope!

Do I always let my light shine? Unfortunately, not.

I am human, and I do make mistakes.

I will be the first to admit that I am not a smiley, happy-go-lucky kind of person. When people first meet me, they think I'm angry. I have that "face," but it's just my look. I got it from my daddy's mother. I never really knew her, but I've seen pictures and she always looked serious or mad, and my mom said that I got it from her. She also said she was a sweet woman, so I hope people will say the same of me, regardless of me always looking mad.

Before we became close friends, my forever best friend once told me that she was terrified of me. She thought I was going to beat her up. I told her I couldn't hurt a fly. After she got to know me, she knew I was a big softy. I can't help who I am, but I am always striving to be better. I have to constantly try to improve who I am.

The reason I have shared so much about myself is because I want people to know I'm not trying to present myself as a positive, flawless, perfect person. I'm human, I have imperfections, and I make mistakes. Sometimes I say things out of anger and lose my cool, and, I admit, I can sometimes be hard to get along with. My husband can testify to that. However, just because we mess up doesn't mean God loves us any less. I have to repent and ask God to forgive me for yelling at people on the road, or for chewing out my husband, or for being rude to people. Just because I want to be a good example for others and live a life that is pleasing to God doesn't mean I won't mess up. God can still use you – in spite of what you've done and what you may do again. He doesn't disqualify you because you have faults or sin or because you might continue messing up. Read His Word. You will find that none of the people God used time and time again were perfect: Moses, David, Peter, Noah. God didn't go around choosing perfect people to be used by Him; He chose the unqualified, the imperfect. This is why I know we all have purpose. We are not perfect people.

I've included some scriptures concerning PURPOSE that have been helpful to me.

I know that you can do all things, and that no thought or purpose of yours can be restrained.
Job 42:2 (Amp)

• • • • • • • • • • • •

And we know that in all things God works for the good of those who love him, who have been called according to his purpose. Romans 8:28

For He delivered us and saved us and called us with a holy calling [a calling that leads to a consecrated life—a life set apart—life of purpose] not because of our works [or because of any personal merit—we could do nothing to earn this] but because of his own purpose and amazing grace [his amazing, undeserved favor] which was granted to us in Jesus Christ before the world began [eternal ages ago]
1Timothy 1:9 (Amp)

Read these scriptures. If you don't understand them, check them out in different translations and pray that God will give you vision and clarity on your PURPOSE.

You have a purpose!

Chapter 10
Letting Go

I'm sure you've heard the expression to "save the best for last." Well, I decided to wait and, in the interest of transparency, tell you the worst of my story at the end. At least, it's what I think is the worst about me. I'm going to be real and tell you some things about my life that are not so nice, some of which I'm not proud of. These are things I've done, ways I've messed up, and times when I chose the wrong path. Some of what I will share with you are things that have been done to me that I've put back into the farthest reaches of my mind. I may not have been the cause of some of those things, but that doesn't mean that I haven't felt shame, guilt, sadness or frustration about these ugly memories. I really don't care to relive these memories or go back to them, but if it means I can help someone, I will go there.

Originally, this wasn't going to be a part of this book. I was going to leave out the "junk" in my life and stay out of my past memories. These are things that I haven't been proud of and a lot of what I've been too embarrassed or ashamed to put it out there. I've been too insecure to let the world know the real me, but God dealt with me about it one morning as I was on my way to work and I have to be obedient. I drive about half an hour to work every day. I use this as my alone time with God. I usually pray every morning on my way to work. Some mornings I listen to sermons on a podcast and other mornings I listen to worship music. During these times, when I have no other distractions besides the cars around me, I have – on more than one occasion – been worshipping and singing and all of sudden God will reveal things to me. Sometimes it's small things. He will put someone in my thoughts, and I will feel the need to pray for them. There have been other times God will show me to forgive someone or remind me that I wasn't right with how I treated someone. This particular morning, I was singing the song, *"No Longer Slaves"* by Bethel Music. This song always grabs my heart and I keep it on my worship music playlist. If you haven't heard it, you should look it up. It talks about not being a slave to fear anymore. As I sang with all my heart, the people passing me on the interstate were probably wondering what was going on in my car! I was singing and worshipping like there was no one else in this world that mattered – because truly, there wasn't! It's during these sweet tender moments that I really don't care who sees me or what they think. They don't know me so who cares if they think I'm nuts? As that song ended, *"Reckless Love"* by Cory Asbury came on. I couldn't contain it anymore. The Holy Spirit was moving so strongly in my car. I heard a voice that said, "It's time to tell your story." I immediately thought, "Oh no! I can't!" Then I heard the Voice say, "You're no longer a slave to fear." Funny how I was just singing that, but fear was already rising up in me. *"Reckless Love"* was still playing and in it, there is a verse that says, "When I felt no worth, You paid it all for me. You have been so, so kind to me." I knew in that instant I had to share my story – even though there are things I didn't want anyone to know.

At this point, I had already started crying and was trying to stay focused on the road. Immediately, negative thoughts started to rise up in me. "What would people think of me? How will they look at me? Will they will see me in a different light?" Then I felt a peace come over me. I remembered I wasn't alone and while this book is <u>about</u> me, it is not <u>for</u> me. God wanted to use it and work through me for His people. I decided I wouldn't hold back. I found my courage and thought to myself, "I'm not going to care anymore about what people think. I haven't been that person in almost 30 years and my one mission is to do God's will and not worry about anything else."

So, if this book only helps one person, then I did my job and most importantly, I was obedient to God. I've prayed for boldness for years so here I go.

Chapter 11
Truth Hurts

Abuse- (verb) to treat in a harmful injurious or offensive way, to speak harshly insultingly and unjustly to or about; (noun) harshly or coarsely insulting language, bad or improper treatment

I will back track a little, but it will be helpful to remember some of the facts I have already included in previous chapters because they will play a big part in this part of my story.

After my parents' separation and with all the moving here and there, a lot of times we stayed for periods of time with family friends or with aunts' and uncles' on my mom's side of the family. This piece of my story started on one occasion when a family member, who was six or seven years older than me, started molesting me. Because I was only about 6 years old, I didn't understand what he was doing to me. I just knew he had me terrified to say anything and always told me that I would be in trouble if I did. I didn't realize I was a victim. Back in those days, it wasn't common for parents to talk to kids about inappropriate touching or that you should tell if it did happen to you. It took me until I was well into my 30's to ever tell my mom - not out of fear anymore - but by that age, it was out of shame and disgust. Actually, it just happened to come out one day as she was sharing something that had happened to her as a kid and before I knew it, I started telling her my story.

I have to admit, though, that he wasn't the only one. I had another distant family member that did things to me, too. I started to hate going to their houses, and to this day, I can get claustrophobic in certain situations. Because the first time I was raped happened at about the age of seven under a bed in his room, the smell of dirty shoes, socks and sweat from a boy's room still haunts me. When I'm closed up in a small elevator or in small, tiny places, it takes me back to those awful memories from when I was a kid and my innocence was taken from me. I get panicked, can't breathe, and totally freak out. I never told anyone about this except my husband. I also shared this with my kids when they were age appropriate; not all the ugly details, but just enough for them to be aware - just in case anyone ever tried to make them victims. I never shared with my brothers or my dad because the wrath of an overprotective brother or daddy would have been bad. I always kept it a secret because we had enough problems and issues with the family and I didn't need to make more waves. At this point, I have gotten over it and have forgiven them. I have let it go, and I would never "throw them under the bus" or "tear up the family" over it. The older I got, I realized that abuse can be a vicious cycle. I found out that they, too, had been sexually abused when they were younger. As I got older, it wasn't as easy to trick me, and I finally started finding ways to avoid being alone with them. By the time I had gotten old enough to tell and talk about it, out of concern that other people might be affected or be victims, I found out he had been to jail several times and he was a having a very rough life. I found out he was paying for a lot of the things he had done. Today, I don't think or dwell on it, I'm not sad or broken about it, I don't harbor hate for myself anymore, or even for the people who did it to me. I learned what to look for and, as a parent, I was very cautious of where my kids went and who they stayed with. I know you can't protect them from everything, but I felt like I could at least try and protect them, based on my experiences and what I had gone through.

I mentioned earlier in the book that because we moved around a lot, it was hard to make friends. In some of those moves, being new to the area and not knowing the people, you actually jump in with the first group that accepts new friends. I have to admit that some of my friend choices may have not been the best. I started drinking at a young age. I was only 12 when I tried my first drink, and an alcoholic drink at that! I tried smoking at that age, too. I never cared for smoking since I had allergies and asthma and being around smoke made it harder to breath. I only did it to fit in with the crowd and to look cool.

In the 7th grade, I was already hearing about girls giving themselves to guys and other things happening. It is, after all, a very hormonal age. I was getting good at drinking and getting drunk, and I actually enjoyed it. What a sad confession for a 12-year-old girl! I did find myself making out with a guy at a party and probably would have been stupid enough to give myself to him because I was so drunk that night. I probably could have been talked into it, but I'm glad I didn't. This wasn't supposed to be a drinking party - it was a middle school party where there was supposed to be dancing, swimming and just hanging out. It was being chaperoned by a few of my friend's parents. The party was being held at my friend's house and she snuck into her dad's liquor stash and got us a bottle of something to drink. Four of us girls drank before everyone else got there, but we didn't let anyone else in on the secret because we didn't want her to get into trouble. I'm not bragging about any of this. It was all stupid, immature choices that I made, and as much as I wish I could, I can't take them back.

I mentioned moving to Wichita Falls when I was 13. My intentions in this part of my story are not to embarrass or blame my parents - only to explain some of the irrational thinking on my part. At NO point in this story do I hold my parents responsible for MY bad choices!

I came from a broken home. Many of you reading this book can relate, but a little bit of back information might help you understand some of my crazy thoughts so I want to share a little bit about each of my parents.

While I love my daddy, he is what can be called a functioning alcoholic. I know that alcoholism can be in your genes, but that cannot be an excuse for one's behavior. Research it and read about it for yourself. I have studied and researched alcoholics for a big part of my life. Alcoholics will say and do things while they are under the influence that they wouldn't normally say or do. It's like two totally different people in one person. I have prayed for my dad for as long as I can remember - for God to heal this disease of alcoholism. I believe one day it will happen, but that is in God's hands and timing. My God is bigger than alcoholism and generational curses.

I love my momma, too, but God knows it took me years to forgive and reconcile with her. Thankfully, we are finally in a good place now, but I saw some real ugliness come from two of the most important people in my life. With my mom, I not only saw alcoholism, I saw drug use and even infidelity. It took me years to get over the fact that she would take me with her to meet a guy and then leave me in a living room full of a bunch of drunks and weirdos. Sometimes she would leave me in that room full of strangers for ten minutes, half an hour, and sometimes longer. My grandma's prayers never failed because, thank God, no one ever tried to hurt me during those times. My mom was out of her mind and didn't know what she was doing. Then she would swear me to secrecy not to tell my dad anything or where we had been. At that early age, my mom was teaching me to lie to my dad. It took me years of hating myself for not telling my dad, but I knew they already had problems and I didn't want to make them worse. Suffice it to say I was one messed up and confused kid.

For years prior to the infidelity, my dad had accused my mom of being unfaithful. She never had been, but one day she said she got tired of the accusations, so she went and did it. It's not a good excuse, but we can all make stupid decisions and then try to make sense of it. I assume my dad grew up with a lot of insecurities himself and must have taken those out on my mom. I remember the words "slut" and "whore" being used a lot - way before the affairs even started. As a kid, I never knew what those words meant. I was young when my parents divorced, and I tried not to remember all the terrible details of my parent's marriage. I only wanted to remember the good memories, but that didn't always happen.

I mentioned my dad's drinking habits for a reason. It's not something I've ever wanted to talk about, but after I moved to Wichita Falls and was around him more often, I started to see things I hadn't seen when I was only there on every other weekend and holiday visits. I knew he drank but I didn't realize how much or how awful it could get. It would get bad enough to where he either passed out or blacked out. He had been in car accidents and had a few DUI's. One time, he had to be pulled from a burning car while he was on one of his drunken episodes. The car was parked and running in front of a Denny's Restaurant. There is no telling how long the car had been running when it burst into flames, but he was passed out inside the car and totally unaware he could have died. A lady saved his life by pulling him out. The car burned down to nothing, but I know God sent that woman who pulled him to safety. I'm sharing this about him not to embarrass him or belittle him. My intent is to stress that he had issues, too, and was dealing with them the only way he knew how. Drinking was his way of coping.

As a teenager in Wichita Falls, I had a middle school boyfriend. God knows nothing ever happened besides the awkward middle school kisses, but my dad would get drunk and accuse me of being a whore or a slut - just like he did my mom. I started thinking, "Does he really think that little of his daughter that he is going to com-pare me to his ex-wife and call me those names?" Girls look up to their daddies for approval, compliments, and protection. Fathers are supposed to build up daughters, not tear them down. I started resenting him a little and, to say the least, I was hurting more than anyone knew. A father is appointed by God to be the head of the house. Even though we weren't a happy home or all under one roof,

I felt like my father was supposed to be building me up, not tearing me down. I didn't dare tell my mom because she would have immediately yanked me out of Wichita Falls, but things weren't much better with her. I felt like I was in a losing situation with both of my parents. I didn't live with my dad but saw him pretty often since we lived in the same town. He was awesome when he was sober, but he was a totally different man when he was drinking. I loved to be around him when he was sober, but when he was drinking I hated it because I never knew what he might say or how he'd say it. I continued to drink and make bad choices, myself. I even tried smoking "weed" a few times. I hated it both times because it made me super sick and dizzy so I never tried it again.

By the time my freshman year came around, I had a different boyfriend. My previous boyfriend and I had broken up because we ended up being more like brother and sister and we realized we didn't really have anything in common. This new boyfriend attended a different high school than me, but was nice and very well-liked by a lot of people. He had my cousins - whom I lived with - fooled because he was clean cut, did well in school, played sports, and was popular. However, what they didn't know is he kept pressuring me for sex all the time. My previous boyfriend never even brought it up. He respected me. My freshman boyfriend was relentless and because we had been dating a while, everyone expected it. My friends were also pressuring me to give in to him because they were all having sex. I finally decided to give myself away, but it was the worst thing I could have ever done. Somehow, I thought it would erase the memories of my childhood and the ugliness of being molested and raped, but all it did was bring back the old emotions and feelings from when I was a kid. My memory was in overdrive with those hurtful memories.

My first thought was, "Well, my dad can finally be right since I decided to have sex, so I guess now, when he tells me not to be whoring around like my mother, it will be on him." My thinking was way off. I was wrong because I wasn't going to admit to anyone that I was having sex - especially not to my parents. I was only hurting myself. It ruined the relationship I had with the guy because from that point on, that's all he ever wanted to do. He wasn't a bad guy, just a normal teenage guy. Still, a piece of me hated both him and me. There was a lot of shame and guilt. Once I had opened that box, it was hard to shut it. I drank even more to numb the pain in my mind. Where does a 14-year-old get alcohol? I got it from friends who had parents with unlocked liquor cabinets or alcohol, wine or beer not being supervised. I was still living with my cousins, who had been kind enough to let me live there, but I think they were noticing I wasn't doing too well. I kept on messing up - one thing after another.

Lie after lie, one mistake after another, it was starting to be a little more than a girl my age could handle. I lied because I had seen so much of it my whole life and it came easy. Some things I lied about because I was trying to make up a life for myself that I wished was more realistic than what my life was really like. After several months of back and forth with this guy, I finally decided to move back with my mom and get away from the mess I had made of myself in Wichita Falls. Thankfully, I only crossed that line with the one guy. It was already a line I wished I hadn't crossed and a mistake I wanted to take back. I never shared with him anything about why I was such a basket case about the whole sex and relationship thing but, honestly, I was too embarrassed for him to know that I had been raped as a kid. Besides, neither one of us were mature enough to have been having sex at age 14. As I said before, I was starting to lie a lot, and I painted a picture of a happy family and a perfect mom and life back in Sulphur Springs. He later found out that wasn't true. Even now, I don't know why I thought it was important for him to think I had this perfect life and family because, had that been true, I never would have left in the first place. I guess I was young and immature, and I had a good imagination.

After I moved back to Sulphur Springs, I told him I had ended up being pregnant with his kid and had an abortion, which was another big fat lie. My mom would never have let me do that. When I left Wichita Falls, he and I were not on the best of terms and it was to the point where I wanted to do or say something to hurt him. I guess what I was looking for was sympathy, or just a way to manipulate him. He felt bad, and we tried to remain friends by letter, but eventually we both moved on and quit writing to each other. It's been 30 years and I think at some point I admitted to him that it was a lie. However, if I didn't, I hope if he ever reads this book, he forgives me. Not for any reason other than I'm striving to be the woman God created me to be and I hate that I lied to him about something that big and that serious, not knowing how that could have affected him.

I look back now and see that when I left Wichita Falls, I didn't really give any one an explanation, other than the fact that my mom needed me after my grandpa's death. That was really just me using that as an excuse to get out and, in some way, run from my problems, like I had always seen my mom do. In just two short years, I had made a mess of my life. All I really knew how to do was to leave when the going got tough.

I do admit that I left with some hurt and unresolved feelings about my dad, but I did what he did best: I buried them, put a pretend smile on my face, and acted like everything was okay. The thing is I felt badly about being upset with him because he never even remembered how ugly he talked or how verbally abusive he was when he got drunk. I have to say though, he never once hit me or got violent; he just said hurtful things. Whoever made up the little saying: "Sticks and stones may break my bones, but words will never hurt me" is a liar! Words *do* hurt, and they stay with us forever. Saying something ugly to someone just one time can continue hurting them for a lifetime, especially if they never find it in their hearts to forgive and forget. That's why it's so important to choose to forgive people. It's not to let those who hurt you off the hook, and it's not saying that what they did was right. However, it can help you release it and not carry the pain so you can live a happy life and not carry frustration, unhappiness and hate.

Earlier, I talked about the summer before my sophomore year. I had done well: attending church and youth church functions regularly for about five or six months. However, after moving back to Sulphur Springs, I started drinking again. It was easily available, and I wanted to fit in. Everyone else was doing it and I thought it was cool and fun. I wish now I could go back in time and tell my younger self how stupid I was being; maybe even give myself a good butt-whipping to get myself in line in order to focus on more important things, but we all know that's impossible. Instead, I have to admit that I made even more irresponsible choices at my young age. I knew a lot of people in Sulphur Springs, so just moving back and having the same friends was the easy part. The difference was that because of my experiences, I had changed. I had the same face and personality, but I had matured in the last few years and it seemed to be gaining me a lot of new attention from the guys. I wasn't crazy about it because, as I stated before, I don't like being the center of attention. It's unnerving when you're being stared at. Some girls get flattered and giggle and flirt. I tried not to make eye contact, would get very uncomfortable and sometimes I would ask, "what the *blank* are you staring at?" Sometimes I would shut down because it would make me feel like I was being undressed with their eyes and against my will, which took me back to the rape from my childhood. I had so many issues back then that probably needed to be dealt with. I never realized until decades later, how much those things from my childhood had affected my life.

I did meet a really nice guy who was a few years older than me. He was a cousin of my best guy friend. He was funny, we got along great and we dated a short while. One night when I was pretty buzzed, I decided to have sex with him. Again, it was not a proud moment for me. I have to say he wasn't like the boyfriend from a year and a half earlier who was always talking about it or trying to pressure me into it. He was a genuinely nice guy and was happy just hanging out and talking, whether we were by ourselves or with friends or family. He had already graduated from high school, so he was ready for a more serious relationship, but I was putting up all kinds of resistance. I was very quiet and standoffish, and I know he was having a hard time reading me and what I wanted. One time, he met some of my family members who had some cute kids and he made the comment, "I wonder what our kids would look like?" I just about had a heart attack! In my mind I thought, "I don't think I ever want to get married!" I had such a messed-up idea of marriage and what marriages were supposed to be like that I didn't want any part of it. One time when we were out with some friends, he hinted about me wearing his class ring. But that night got messed up because the couple we went with got into a huge argument and fought all evening. We pretty much felt their tension and it ruined our night, when we said our goodbyes that night, I wasn't disappointed; I was more relieved that he didn't ask me to wear his class ring. Being around that couple's arguing had brought back memories of the jacked-up relationships I was used to seeing, which reinforced the fact that I didn't want any part of that. We continued to see each other and hang out, but I don't think we wanted the same things. To top it off, I was very insecure because he had several girls after him. He never made me feel like he wanted anyone else, but I couldn't ever get past the fact that I didn't think I was good enough for him. I got busy and started missing a lot of his calls and he probably thought I was avoiding him. The dating with him finally came to an end but, to be honest, it worked out the way it was supposed to because he wasn't who God had for me. My mind always kept me defeated and insecure. I always felt like I wouldn't amount to anything, and I even believed I didn't deserve happiness, even though every one of my friends thought I had it all together. In actuality, what they thought was confidence was really just a huge front. Inside, I had a hard time ever imagining a happily-ever-after for me because in my world – that just didn't exist.

That is truly what I thought then, but a few months after that guy and I quit dating, I met Rob. I already told you the story of how we met, fell in love, dated, and married. A few months previously, I could never have imagined a marriage and kids but once the right person was put in my life, the whole image of marriage changed in my mind. That is the miracle of love.

Rob is the love of my life and we've had 28 wonderful years together. He has always been there for me through thick and thin. We have grown up together, he knows how to read me and how to love me, even at times when I can't love myself. Even in our minor disagreements, he is still the love of my life, and is still the only person with whom I want to grow old. Happy marriages can happen and do exist - despite what I had always thought and seen modeled.

I won't lie and say all of our married life has been candy and roses. Two people put together from broken and jacked-up home-lives is not a great combination. We have argued, disagreed a lot and have said things we wished we could take back. Our early years were very hard. Growing up, I was taught (and saw) that it was easy to get up and leave when things got tough and I threatened to do just that several times during those first few years. Things were hard, we were young, neither of us had grown up in the best environments or with the best examples, and we were financially strapped. When you're starting out, that's a rough combination. My husband would get mad, but got over the arguments quickly. He wasn't a quitter or a runner. He is a hard-headed, persistent person and he wouldn't let me quit or run when things got tough. He would make sure, once we calmed down, that we talked and worked it out. It's one of the many things I love about him. I'm glad he always made me calm down and think things through. He taught me that we don't run away from our problems. We have grounded each other and have learned so many things from each other in the last 28 years.

So - back to even more ugly truths. My mom did the best she could, but she was physically abusive. If we back-talked her, if we rolled our eyes or used a tone she didn't agree with, we were slapped - sometimes in the face. We were pushed, shoved, yelled at, and a few times a fist or two would be waved in front of our faces. I never got hit with a fist, but I can say she waved it at me a few times, and on several occasions, I was slapped because I never knew when to shut up. I kept on arguing, especially in my middle school years when I knew I was right.

My mom got really messed up during my middle school years. I know she was involved in drugs and that caused her to lose her identity. Though I don't know what kind of drugs they were, I do know they changed her. The following story is one example of my life with mom during this time. My dad paid child support but we were living at poverty level with mom so we qualified for government help. Mom had us on free lunches and anything else that we could get free, but I was too proud to use it. I didn't want to be the kid in line with the free lunch tickets when all of my friends had cash. I was afraid of what they would think of me. Oh, the pressures of being a middle school teenager! So, at school, if I didn't have cash to eat, I would just say I wasn't hungry. I finally admitted this to my dad, and he started mailing a separate money order specifically addressed to me. He sent me $20 every two weeks so I could have the school lunch, and sometimes he would send me extra money so I could go do things with my friends. However, my mom didn't know my dad was sending me money. I always had my aunt cash it with my uncle at a local business that he ran because I didn't have a way to get to a bank. Besides, I was minor without an ID so it was hard to cash the money orders. My dad didn't want to send cash because he wanted to make sure I would receive it, and he didn't trust my mom. It was a good set up because then I had cash for lunches and I was like everyone else.

One day, my aunt slipped and mentioned the money order to my mom. When my mom came home late that evening, she asked if she could borrow some of my lunch money. I was good at hiding things and I had hidden the cash in a pair of old shoes. I told my mom I didn't have any cash, but she knew I was lying. She yelled and slapped me, then started digging through all my personal property. She would go back to being nice and say, "I'll pay you back," but I couldn't make myself believe her. I knew if I gave it to her I wouldn't ever see it again, which meant me starving for another two weeks at school. I know that was my pride, because I had a way to eat by being on the free lunch program, but this was my money that my dad sent specifically for me. When I didn't back down, she went back to being mean and screaming. On this occasion, she pinned me up against the wall in my closet and was choking me. The only thing that saved me was my little brother crying, screaming and begging for her to stop. She finally let go and left with her husband. I suppose they needed a fix and that's why she was so desperate.

Even though you may not intend to repeat some of your parent's mistakes or how they raised you, there are times - without even trying - you realize that more of their raising was ingrained in you than you thought. In 1996, I was pregnant with my daughter, very hormonal and sick. On this particular day, my son, who was three, was playing with a new Spiderman we had bought for him. Even though we lived in a rent house, we always took care of wherever we lived as if it were our own. I had been cleaning house that day and my son had been playing and entertaining himself in his room. When I walked into the hallway to go peek in on him, I noticed some large red marks all over the wall. I was immediately livid! My husband had been outside mowing but had come inside to cool off or drink some water. I don't recall the exact details of why he was back inside the house, but he was inside. We didn't allow our son the freedom to have crayons or markers unless he was sitting at the table, so I knew the marks were not crayon marks. Immediately after I walked into his room, he started showing me something about this new Spiderman but I wasn't listening. All I could do was interrupt him and ask him if he knew what the marks were. He sheepishly said, "No, Mommy." I said, "Son, you are lying. What is this?" He said, "I don't know." My son wouldn't look at me and I knew by the way he was acting that he was lying. I said, "You better tell me what this is!" He again said, "I don't know." Somehow, a switch flipped inside my brain. Suddenly, I was over in front of him and reached down and slapped him one time on the cheek. Immediately, I saw the pain and hurt in his eyes and I instantly wanted to die. He quickly admitted that it was the red feet of the Spiderman figure that he had used to make the marks on the wall. I wanted a confession, but at this point he was crying and I was already beginning to tear up because it had clicked. I had slapped him in the same way my mom used to slap me, even though I had always said I would never hit my kids in the face like that. I didn't hit him hard enough to leave a mark, but it upset me tremendously that I had left a mark in his mind and on his heart. I know it hurt him emotionally because I remember how it always hurt me when I was slapped. The slap always stung, but the heart-ache was even worse. The multitudes of heartbreak from my mom all came rushing back. My husband heard the commotion and came rushing in to see what had taken place. I knew I had done wrong and I wanted to take it back. My husband made things worse by saying, "Melissa, I love you and I know you were brought up like that; but we do not discipline our son in that way. Spank him in the right way if it's necessary, but you will never hit my son like that again." He repeated, "Do you understand me? You will never hit my son like that again." I nodded yes, because I couldn't talk from the knot in my throat. I knew he was absolutely right. I had messed up. I grabbed my son and hugged him and we both cried in each other's arms. I told him I was sorry. I told him that Mommy would never hit him like that ever again. He told me he was sorry. He didn't like lying to me and he wouldn't lie to me again. He's 25 now and he will tell you - I never slapped him again. I kept my promise to him. I wanted to break that nasty, abusive curse. I found out years later that my grandma used to hit her kids with extension cords or anything else she could grab that might have been nearby when her kids had done something wrong and she was trying to discipline them. My mom corrected us in the only way she knew how, but when you mix that with drugs and whatever else was going on in her life, it made it worse on us as her kids.

I am not proud of that moment, but I believe that explanation is relevant to my story in a lot of ways. We sometimes do things to our kids that we have either seen or were brought up watching. The only way we know how to parent is by the examples we saw growing up. I am not going to say our kids didn't get spanked if they did wrong, but we did it in a calm manner and not out of anger. They turned out to be great kids, respectful teenagers, responsible young people, and now hard-working adults of whom I am very proud.

I can't say they were perfect little angels all the time, but we never had discipline problems with them in school. They always respected their elders and they knew how to act. Individually, we all have to break off past habits, behaviors, and patterns. We can't pass those things on to our future generations. I see how our son is with our grandson. He is loving and patient. He does get onto him when it is necessary, but he does it in a loving manner, and it warms my heart that he's such a great father. I think, "Who is this man standing before me?" I thank God for the children He blessed me with and that they turned out so good. Because of the families that Rob and I came from, our kids could have turned out so differently and so messed up, even worse than we were! But thank God, He turned our lives around and faced us in the right direction to raise some awesome adults. Our daughter is now expecting and I can't wait to see her with her son! I know she will be an amazing momma.

Even though I know he's forgiven me, admitting that I hit my son breaks my heart all over again. I've never really shared that with anyone besides my mom. We both cried when I told her. I cried because it's still not something I like to remember, even though it only happened the one time. My mom cried because she understood the damage she had done in my life. I don't want people to judge or hate my mom (or anyone mentioned in this book) because I have personally let go of the hurts and have forgiven her. Although if took a lot of years to get to this point, we have a great relationship now. It also took God to change my heart and the relationship I had with Him to cause a shift in me. The change He made in me gave me the desire to start forgiving those people who had hurt me. It's never too late to reconcile with your parents or loved ones! Don't waste time harboring hate and anger.

I said I had to let go of **insecurity**. Part of my insecurity stemmed from watching how my mom had cheated on my dad and how badly it had hurt him. In my heart, I didn't want to take a chance and get hurt.

I also mentioned that I had to let go of **hate**. I harbored hate for my mom for what she had done to me and how she had treated my dad for years. I hated the family member who had raped me and the one who molested me. I had let hate build up inside of me for all those years in school that I had been picked on when we moved from town to town and I was the new kid. I hated myself for the mistakes I had made and for things I had done that I couldn't change or take back. For so many years, I didn't like who I had turned into.

One Sunday at church, I heard a sermon about **forgiveness** and how I could be a happier person if I learned to forgive. After that sermon, the next time my dad came to visit was in 2011. I sat down with my parents in my dining room and I poured my heart out. I told them that I was choosing to forgive them and I told them exactly what I needed to forgive them for. I asked them to forgive me if I had ever done anything to hurt them. This was the beginning of reconciliation for us. I haven't seen or spoken to those family members that had hurt me in years, but I gave it to God and told him I didn't want to hate them anymore. I wholeheartedly let it all go. I do have to say: the Word of God is true! It was amazing how quickly I felt at peace! I didn't have that uneasy feeling around my parents anymore. No longer did I have the feeling that I wasn't good enough. I started feeling more confident and I felt like a weight had been lifted off of me.

There are so many things in my life I wish I could change or do over. I wish I could repair mistakes that I have made, but only God knows why they happened the way they did and what purpose it has served in my life. He does say He can and will use all things in our lives for good(Romans 8:28).

There are so many times that bad things could have happened, either to me or to some of my close friends. An example of this happened a year before I started dating Rob. I remember driving around and being followed by some out of town guys in a really cool sports car. They asked Nora and I to get in their car and go riding around. Nora parked her car and we got in with them, even though we didn't know them. We just thought, "Hey, they are cute. Let's go!" That was stupid and dangerous. We went around the main drag once with these guys until some of our close guy friends saw us and chased us down. They flashed their lights, made the guys pull over, and forced us to get out of the car. Then they chewed us out for getting in a car with total strangers. One of our guy friends said, "You girls could have been raped or killed! What were you thinking?" The fact is - we weren't thinking! We just thought these older guys from out of town were good looking. It never once crossed my mind that they might try to hurt us. They seemed harmless.

I remember another instance during my sophomore year when we went to a club in Greenville to listen my friend, Dave's, step-dad sing in a country and western band. This place always stamped us as minors, so Nora and I always went straight to the bathroom to wash off the stamp. We looked and dressed older so, of course, cowboys would buy us drinks and ask us to dance. Of the several times we went, there was one particular night when we all got super drunk. Nora drove us there, but she was feeling sick, Dave had drunk too much and the other guy we had brought, Brad, was throwing up. We were all drunk, to say the least. Remember I said alcohol didn't make me sick? It did, however, make me feel braver – like I was 10-feet tall and invincible. Honestly, it caused me to make more stupid decisions. We all had curfews and so I was designated as the one who had to get us back to Sulphur Springs. I didn't have a real license, only a learner's permit, and I had never driven on the interstate, just on the service roads. Nevertheless, since I was voted to do the job and I wasn't about to tell my friends, who needed me at this time, "No!" I can't believe we didn't get pulled over! I remember driving way too slowly for the interstate because one of them kept having to puke. My vision of the road was blurry because I hadn't worn my glasses to go out. Without them I couldn't see clearly and since I hadn't driven over there, I didn't take them with me. There were so many decisions like that in my life. Over and over, one poor decision after another, but I feel like God was always with me - even in my stupidity. I didn't see it or recognize it then, but I know and understand now, there are so many times things could have turned out badly for me, but by God's saving grace, His protection, and my Grandma's prayers, they didn't.

My ugly truths are not only about being verbally and physically abused, molested, raped, lied to, taught how to lie at an early age. I've also been bullied, picked on, ostracized, gossiped about, had lies made up about me, and so many other things. I could actually go on all day with story after story of the many things from which I've been healed, things from which God has protected me, and other situations where I walked away untouched … but I won't.

I'm not the only who has stories to share. Everyone has a story, a testimony, a life-changing experience, but some of you may never tell it. Some of you are trapped inside your past and can't be happy or think about the future because you can't get out of the past. Pastor Michael Todd says it this way. "The past is the prison of your present but it's the torment of your potential future. If you live in the past, your present is frustrated and your future is nonexistent." I tell my story because I want people to understand that what I've laid out here isn't for me to boast. It's not about me remembering my past memories as good times or fun times or to brag about being lucky in some instances and not getting caught. It's not to flaunt how bad I was and the things I may have gotten away with. I want to tell my life story and share these things for one purpose and only: to remind myself - and you - how good God is! He loves us no matter what!

Recently, Pastor Bryan Sparks said something that really struck a chord in me., "We should never forget that we are all here because of the grace, mercy and love of God. There are things in your past that you need to forget forever, and there are things in your past you should never forget. Most of us remember what we should forget, and we forget what we should remember." He said, "We shouldn't remember the things in our past to remind ourselves of how bad we were. We should remember our past to remind ourselves and others of how good God is."

THAT is exactly the purpose of me writing this book.

He also included this scripture,

But watch out! Be careful never to forget what
you yourself have seen. Do not let those memories
escape from your mind as long as you live! And be
sure to pass them on to your children and grand-
children. Deuteronomy 4:9(NLT)

I thought, "That is so good, I have to include that in my book!" I want to leave this book for my children and grandchildren as a reminder of God's amazing grace and love. My memories sometimes make me sad, but then I start to talk about it or remember the final outcome and it always brings me joy when I'm reminded of how good God has been to me.

Chapter 12
find your Purpose

In closing, I want to tell you this: <u>Find your purpose!</u>

As I was listening to a sermon on a podcast by Pastor Steven Furtick, I heard the following statement. It definitely made an impression on me.

> Purpose <u>isn't </u>money, or big houses, or elaborate vacations.
>
> Purpose <u>is</u> what we were created to do.
>
> If we can get to purpose, it doesn't matter who or what comes against you.

Remember, God has already equipped us with everything we need to find our purpose and for us to do what He has created us to do. I wish there was a way I could help everyone and tell them what their purpose is. Unfortunately, I can't. However, I can say this: if you dive into God's Word and seek Him daily, you will be able to more clearly find and understand your purpose. I know this is isn't easy to do. I still find it hard to make time to read the Bible, and there are things about it I don't always understand. Some books in the Bible are definitely harder than others, but we have it easier today with technology. We can access the Bible on our phones and iPads and Apple Watches. We don't have to remember to take our

Bible with us. Wherever you carry your phone, you already have access to it. You can even read it on your work break or at lunch, and there are many different versions and translations from which to choose.

Reading God's Word is important because it can start to come alive in front of you. It helps you. It's like a tool - a weapon of sorts - to help you get through your everyday life. At first, it may be hard. When I first started, I remember trying to read, but sometimes I got so lost and confused, the wording would totally bewilder me. When I started pulling it up on my phone and read the Word in different translations, I was like "Okay…. I get it! That makes more sense." The Amplified and The Passion translation really break it down for me. They are so much easier to understand because they are in "today's" terminology! There are also some really good study Bibles out there that can break the scriptures down for you and help you understand.

Not only reading the Bible but having some alone time or quiet time with God can also make a huge difference in one's life. Some people use a prayer "closet" (which is really just a place where you can be alone and without distractions), some pray in the shower, and some people pray in their cars. Where you choose to pray doesn't matter - just make it a point to give God time. It could be two minutes, or 20 minutes, or even two hours, depending on what you need to talk to God about. It's a personal relationship and communication with Him, like you would have with any person. When you start speaking to Him daily and giving Him time, you will hear Him start speaking to you. It's not a loud, thunderous earth-shaking voice. It's comforting and tender and, trust me, you will know. It's hard to explain how it works, but it does work. "My sheep hear my Voice" (John 10:27).

Do this for yourself. Invest in time with God. Try it for 30 days and I promise you, by the second week, you will already start to feel different about how you see things. You will have a hunger for God like never before. You will have more of a loving heart for people, and you will start to see things turn around for you that you could never have imagined. He will start changing you from the inside out.

Marriages will be restored, broken relationships with family members will start to heal, and you will have more courage to openly pray for those around you who are hurting. A personal relationship with Him can help you know and recognize those who need Jesus and who need a touch from Him. You will be more of aware of the lost and hurting world. I can't explain all the goodness that comes from just taking that first step.

As you begin to make a closer relationship with Him a priority in your life, don't expect your life to suddenly be all easy and glorious. As a matter of fact, when you decide to change things in your life, your own life may get a little more challenging. That is because our enemy is going to be mad, and he will try to put up obstacles and bring things to discourage you. He will mess with your mind and say, "Look how hard you're trying and everything around you is falling apart. He will try to defeat you in your mind and emotions. He is going to try to make you feel like your relationship with God isn't worth it - but don't relent! He might try to challenge you in your finances, or in your marriage, or your kids might start rebelling. You will know you're doing right when things start falling by the way-side. Trust me, it will only be for a season. Hang in there and stay strong! God has you.

Don't give up! Remember, God always wins! And He always has the last word! If God is for you, who can be against you (Romans 8:31). Keep in mind that anytime things come against you, it is just a tactic from the enemy to keep you distracted from your God-given purpose.

Make sure to claim his Word and His promises daily:

No weapon formed against you will prosper. Isaiah 54:17

. . . .

I can do all things through Christ who strengthens me. Philippians 4:13

. . . .

The Spirit of God who raised Jesus from the dead lives in you. Romans 8:11

. . . .

Rejoice in the Lord always. Philippians 4:4

. . . .

Fight the good fight of faith. 1 Timothy 6:12

. . . .

He comforts us in all our troubles so that we can comfort others. 2 Corinthians 1:4

. . . .

The Lord himself will fight for you. Just stay calm. Exodus 14:14

. . . .

The Lord is my rock, my fortress, my deliverer. Psalm 18:2

. . . .

Cast all your anxiety on him, because he cares for you. 1 Peter 5:7

I don't have all the answers or an easy way to tell you how to get to your purpose. I can only share from my life what has worked for me. If it works for me, I know it can and will work for you.

Find your purpose!

About the Author

Melissa Ford is a wife, mother, and "Hunny" (grandma name). During the time she wrote the book, she was working a full-time job but spent a lot of her free time writing. When she has spare time available now, she enjoys reading and spending time with her family. She is an active member of One Church in Caddo Mills Texas, and she loves her church and community group families.

Melissa was brought up going to church regularly and was introduced to having a relationship with God at a very young age. However, she experienced some difficult times in her life where she questioned her faith. She went through some rebellious years but could never quite run away from God. She is thankful that God never gave up on her - and that she has learned to never give up on God.

After she became a mother, something in her changed. She began to understand and intrinsically know that the only way she could get through this life successfully and be the mom and wife she wanted to be was to grab hold of God with everything she had. She hasn't let go and continues to grow her faith in the hopes that she can be a good example for her kids and for the generations to come in her family.

Melissa was born in Wichita Falls, Texas, but has lived most of her life in Sulphur Springs, Texas. She and her husband reside in a small town in East Texas and are enjoying their empty nest. In 2017, Melissa had the honor of becoming a grandmother to her first grandson and in 2019 was blessed with her second grandson. She loves the time she gets with the boys, and she has fun spoiling them. Grandbabies are a wonderful blessing from God.

References

Page 7 definition of purpose: Webster's dictionary

Page 24 definition of divorce: Webster's dictionary

Page 119 definition of abuse: Webster's dictionary

Page 25 Statistics information: www.fatherhood.org statistics and free resources. The proof is in the fact that the father's absence harms children

Pages 8, 9, 13, 15, 22, 52, 72, 84, 91, 100, 101, 102, 103, 104, 114, 115, 141, 145, 146, 147 have scriptures from The Bible: translations include NIV, AMP, NLT & The Passion Translation

Page 140 Some information that I heard Pastor Michael Todd say on one of his podcasts. (Pastor at Transformation Church Tulsa Oklahoma)

Page 141 Some information that I wrote down from one of my pastor's sermons- (Pastor Bryan Sparks at One Church Caddo Mills, Texas)

Page 143 Some information that I heard Pastor Steven Furtick say on one of his podcast. (Pastor at Elevate Church)